Surviving Seminars
A Humorous Self-Help Guide

by Randy Segler

Available at Books-a-Million

Surviving Seminars: A Humorous Self-Help Guide © 1999 by Randy Segler.

All rights reserved. Written permission must be secured from the publisher to use or reproduce any part of this book except for brief quotations in critical reviews or articles.
For information, write
The Surviving Stuff Company, Post Office Box 15655, Panama City, Florida 32406-5655.

Printed in the United States of America.
Published by Boulevard Books, Inc. of Florida,
1016 Buena Vista Boulevard, Panama City, Florida 32401.
Distributed by The Surviving Stuff Company.

ISBN 1-882444-10-08

ATTENTION BUSINESSES:

This book is available at quantity discounts with bulk purchase for educational, business, or sales promotional use. For information write The Surviving Stuff Company at the address above.

DEDICATION

This book is dedicated to everyone who has endured a seminar and persevered.

ACKNOWLEDGEMENTS

Bobby Barton, Mike Potter, and especially Clyde Olson for their equally warped senses of humor and encouragement.

Kay Mulligan Judah, Cande McNeil, and Wadona Riley for their review and input.

Beki Comins and Melissa West for helping get the commas in the right place.

Table of Contents

Preface

Introduction … 1

Standard Elements … 5

  Travel … 6
  Weather … 8
  Airlines … 9
  Ground Transportation … 11
  Lodging … 12
  Food … 14
  Facilities … 16
    The Hotel … 16
    Food … 18
    The Bar … 19

Characters … 20
  Seminar Coordinator … 20
  Seminar Planner … 22
  Presenters … 24
    Flatliner … 24
    Drill Sergeant … 26
    The Comedian Wannabe … 28
    Fog Horn … 30
    Church Mouse … 32
    Mr. Acronym … 34
    Last Minute Fill-In … 36
    Brand New Speaker … 38
  Participants … 40
    Seminar Groupies … 40
    Know-It-All … 42
    Clueless One … 44
    Oat Sower … 46
    Hunk … 48
    Party Animal … 50
    Miss Perky … 52
    Wall Flower … 54
    Idea Monger … 56

Presentation Styles & Methods … 58
  Humor … 60
  Cliché Link … 62
  Stream of Consciousness … 64
  Rhetorical Questions … 66
  Perpetual Plot … 68
  Questions At The End … 70
  TV Production … 72
  Handouts … 74
  Charts And Graphs … 76
  Easels And Magic Markers … 78

Overheads	80
Slides	82
Computer Presentations	84
Videos	86
Stupid Name Game	88
Audience Involvement	90
Group Projects	92
Panel of Experts	94

Physical Conditions — 97

Severe Bladder Tension (SBT)	98
Sugar Coma	99
Caffeine Frenzy	100
Hangover	101
Terminal Boredom	102
Restraint Deficiency	103
Forehead Slumber Rash (FSR)	104
Eyelid Droop	105
Tailbone Tingle (TT)	106
Cerebral Relocation	107

Tools & Techniques — 109

Seating Strategy	110
Clothing Strategy	115
Alertness Simulation	117
Destroying Speaker Confidence	118
Dead Donkey Indicator	119
Debilitating Questions	120
Scorecard for Jokes	122
UH Scorecard	122
Speaker Rating Scorecard (SRS)	123
Charisma Barometer	126
Egometer	127
Rate of Speech (ROS)	128
UH Factor	130
Visual Aid Usage	132
Average Boredom Level (ABL)	133
Table Top Gravitation	137
Quantum Logic Leaps	140
Dead Donkey Factor	141
Topic Excitement Score	142
Hand Signals	144
Useless Binder Collections	146
Insuring Future Attendance	147

Glossary — 149

Afterward — 159

About the Author

Coming Soon

PREFACE

Several years ago, I sat in yet another seminar listening to yet another speaker drone on about the subtle nuances of yet another regulatory change. I was irritated that my boss had sent me to another one of these things. The session was excruciatingly boring and I do not deal particularly well with boredom. I decided to write my own satirical review of the speaker and of the seminar. Then I made a list of ways the program could be sabotaged. Soon it was difficult to keep from chuckling out loud. (Admit it...you've done it too.) Suddenly, my aggravation was gone and my focus returned to the important, though still not interesting, material.

Over the next several years, this technique made many other seminars and conferences bearable. Patterns began to emerge and soon it was clear that a book was needed to present my collection of findings and "solutions". More importantly, a book was needed to share how humor could remove irritations and redirect attention to the real issues.

This book, and others to come in the Surviving Stuff Series, is designed to be easy to read, to help find humor in our common experiences and to use that humor to cope with challenges. Sometimes the best solution to a problem lies not in taking action, but in altering our view of the situation or person. This book describes common situations in comical terms and then explores the reckless, irresponsible things we would love to do in response and the more rational solutions we ought to pursue. It is targeted to the neophyte seminar attendee but is relevant to seasoned seminar survivors as well.

One final note...Though many of the observations in this book came from real life experiences, the situations and characters described are composites. No single individual or situation is included in the books because that would limit its relevance. It's my hope that you will laugh long and hard reading this book. Then I hope that you will laugh, cope better, and learn more each time you attend a seminar.

Randy Segler

Surviving Seminars:

INTRODUCTION

"So that's what it's all about!"

A Humorous Self-Help Guide

INTRODUCTION

Surviving Seminars is about full-fledged seminars, which include the following elements:

- participants traveling from various locations via commercial transportation,

- at least two full days of sessions,

- a large binder of largely useless information to which participants will never again refer but which they will prominently display in their workplaces,

- a collection for participants of worthless trinkets advertising a variety of firms which may or may not have any relevance to the seminar, and

- a written evaluation of the seminar to help perpetuate its existence.

INTRODUCTION

Surviving Seminars was developed to help first time seminar attendees understand what they will experience. It was also written to help seasoned seminar survivors reflect on (OK...laugh about) their adventures. It's about recognizing absurdity when you see it, dreaming up ways to combat it, laughing about them, and then pursuing a more responsible course of action.

Solutions recommended in most of the book resulted from exhausting (not to be confused with exhaustive) research over twenty years. You will quickly realize that many of the possible solutions described are for your amusement only. They are designed to help you keep the frustration in perspective by dreaming about what you would love to do (but, hopefully, never will).

Book sections include *Standard Elements, Physical Conditions, Tools & Techniques,* and a *Glossary*. Legitimate advice can be found in the *Afterward*.

INTRODUCTION

In the *Standard Elements* section, seasoned seminar survivors will recognize things present in all seminars. Things like the facilities, characters, and presentation styles, not to mention the food. Included are ways to turn bothersome annoyances into emotionally satisfying experiences.

Physical Conditions gives descriptions of potentially debilitating seminar afflictions participants may face. There are details on avoiding these conditions, treating them if you fail to avoid them, and in some cases, how to inflict them on others.

The *Tools & Techniques* section provides ways you can strategically and effectively approach seminar survival. These range from simple speaker rating scorecards to elaborate statistical measurement of seminar events and techniques for debilitating speakers.

The *Glossary* will help you interpret seminar lingo. (Duh!)

Finally, the *Afterward* provides advice you might actually want to use. It covers how to get the most from your seminar by laughing at the nonsense, focusing on the substance, and building contacts.

STANDARD ELEMENTS

"It's deja vu all over again"

STANDARD ELEMENTS

TRAVEL

With the arrival of the first participants, a familiar ritual begins. It is an icebreaker for people meeting each other for the first time and for old friends. It is a rite of passage for the neophyte attendee. It is a competition.

Sometimes it begins at the first session. Sometimes it begins in the lounge. Sometimes it begins at the registration desk. Sometimes it even starts at the airport or in the cab to the hotel. But it always begins.

Tentatively at first, then with increasing gusto, participants start sharing stories about how they got there and how *bad* it was. How many people were overbooked for their flight. How many babies were on the plane. How obnoxious the person beside them was. How bad the weather was. How many engines failed during flight. How long it took to get transportation to the hotel. How heavy or bulky their luggage was (as if this was someone else's fault!)

STANDARD ELEMENTS

If they didn't have any difficulty arriving, then virtually everyone is compelled to recall a previous bad experience. The stories go on and on. Much like the fisherman's lost catch, stories grow as the seminar progresses. Not only do previous situations get worse, but new hotel horrors are added.

Once in a while a brave soul will venture into the fray describing a pleasant experience. One of two things will happen. The whole tone of the discussion will change to positive experiences. Or reality. The brave soul will forever regret their decision to share, as countless rebuttals are offered challenging the possibility that this occurred.

The Travel Horror Stories generally are about weather, flights, ground transportation, lodging and/or food. Some typical things that you will hear from other Travel Warriors are described in the next few pages.

STANDARD ELEMENTS

WEATHER

For some unknown reason, everyone loves to talk about the times they traveled in poor weather conditions. The worse the conditions, the more dynamic the story and the storyteller. The stories feed on each other and might begin with a simple statement like "It was raining cats and dogs when I arrived at the airport."

This gets elevated to graphic descriptions of flight turbulence, ice on the wings or extreme heat (which always leads to discussion about no air conditioning while the plane sat on the runway), rerouted flights, and missed connections.

Eventually the conversation gets escalated to incredible descriptions of in-flight views from inside a tornado and lightening passing through the body of the traveler. This may lead you to question why the idiot was travelling in those conditions in the first place, or to speculate on the integrity of the story.

STANDARD ELEMENTS

AIRLINES

No mode of transportation provides more ammunition for Travel Warriors than the airlines. Virtually everyone who flies has had at least one bad experience and they love to tell about it or them. To help you sort out the mere whiners from the truly victimized, use the following method to score travel horror stories. Don't let them know you are scoring or the stories might expand-Travel Warriors can be a lot like fishermen.

- **Flight schedules** – Award one Travel Horror Mile (THM) for schedules beginning before dawn or after dinner. Award another mile if the schedule left a short connection...say less than an hour in Hartsfield (Atlanta) with a concourse change.

- **Overbooking** – Award one mile if their flight was overbooked. Award two additional miles if they got bumped from their flight due to overbooking and a short connection which kept them from arriving before their seat was given away.

- **Passengers** – Award one mile for each offensive passenger described. Award double miles if the Travel Warrior was sandwiched between offensive passengers.
- **Cost** – Deduct one point for a complaint about high cost resulting from last minute

STANDARD ELEMENTS

booking unless the last minute direction came from the boss.

- **Number of changes** – Award one mile for the first connecting flight and two miles for each additional connection during a single one-way trip. This only applies if plane changes are involved.

- **Food** – Award one point ONLY if something extraordinary happens like not getting served or like Nuns having a food fight. Award two miles if no food was served on the flights and tight connections caused the Travel Warrior to go more than five hours without nourishment.

- **Luggage requirements** – Award one mile for complaints about excessive luggage by other passengers. Award a bonus mile if the Travel Warrior has the courage to admit that they carried too much on the flight.

- **Lost luggage** – Award five miles for luggage that is a day late arriving. This only happens when people travel in clothes entirely inappropriate for the seminar.

GROUND TRANSPORTATION

As if the flights didn't provide enough material for travel horror stories, Travel Warriors have to collect their luggage (if it arrived) and run through the gauntlet of smokers, who have been banished from the terminal, to reach the various forms of ground transportation. There they will find a veritable plethora of transportation choices ranging from shuttles, to cabs, to limousines, to rickshaws.

Thrifty passengers, and those with cheap bosses, will call the hotel for the free shuttle and then stand waiting for a Federally required minimum of thirty minutes. This provides the opportunity to experience the sights and sounds of the city while inhaling the sweet smell of diesel fumes and cigarette smoke. Some passengers will get in line to be hurtled through the city in a cab with no seat belts by a non-English speaking driver who miraculously (and sometimes circuitously) delivers them to their destination. Others will ride buses with numerous other overburdened passengers to make the 60-mile journey to the car rental facilities. A lucky few will have avoided all this because a limousine driver stood with their name on a card as they emerged from the luggage redistribution area.

STANDARD ELEMENTS

LODGING

The exhaustive pre-registration form that you complete allows the Seminar Planners to build a personality profile of you. They do this to insure that everything about your stay will be perfect. Unfortunately, the less than forthright information you provided combined with the cheap profile building software resulted in a less than accurate picture. This leads to a less than perfect experience.

Starting with the bed, your accommodations will be exactly the opposite of what you like at home. If you like to float in a cushion of padding you'll get the plywood mattress. If lots of support is your thing, you'll get the Grand Canyon mattress with deep chasms in the middle. The pillows almost always fall into two categories, cotton-clad watermelons, or limp bags containing exactly two down feathers. If you are a non-smoker, you will be able to detect immediately that despite the non-smoker room designation, someone smoked there one night in 1972.

No matter what your profile said, the walls in your room will be paper-thin, permitting you to hear everything happening in the adjoining room. This includes the blaring television being used to put them to sleep (which stays on all night) or to mask other activity.

Requesting a room change will only annoy the staff and you will be placed in a room that is nearly silent until the elevator moves.

Nicer hotels now provide a coffee maker with complimentary sealed packages of what is supposedly regular and decaffeinated coffee grounds. These packages have no expiration date because the calendar was still in development when they were packaged. The resulting beverage will wake you up but be careful which way you face when you take the first sip. The involuntary spray could stain your clothes or important documents.

In the old European cities, people threw trash out their windows into trenches below. It was picked up or swept away later. This tradition continues today in hotels. Since the windows only open to a scenic view of the parking garage (people paying non-seminar rates get the good views), room service trays are tossed into the hallways. You may notice a correlation between rooms with these rubbish piles and televisions blaring.

STANDARD ELEMENTS

FOOD

People will complain about the convenience of outrageously priced, bad food delivered to the room at almost any hour of the day or night (except when you arrive late and hungry). They will also complain about the same expensive, bad, but slightly warmer, food served by the hotel at cleverly named restaurants with well-designed menus. The service at these restaurants lives up to the lofty standards you would expect from a restaurant with no hopes of getting business from anyone except hotel guests without rental cars. But they have the benefit of allowing you to charge the meals directly to your exorbitant hotel bill.

Hotels also provide this same food, adapted for seminar budgetary concerns, in group settings to help expand opportunities for participant interaction. This leads to the exchange of valuable information like:

- "That was too much bad food."
- "Those sure were bad appetizers. When do we get the bad meal?"
- "That food was too spicy." (Usually followed by a description of the digestive implications)
- "That bad food was too bland." (Usually followed by a list of favorite herbs and spices)

STANDARD ELEMENTS

- "The presentation of that bad food was too pretty."
- "That bad food needed more parsley to dress it up."
- "They sure have a lot of recipes for chicken."
- "One can never get enough chicken."
- "My soup is too hot."
- "This frozen chicken is too cold."

Goldilocks never attends seminars.

STANDARD ELEMENTS

FACILITIES

THE HOTEL

Most full-fledged seminars take place in large expensive hotels with conference facilities. The meetings take place in huge ballrooms with immense plastic chandeliers, neutral colored walls and carpet that you would never allow in your home. Sometimes, your group is not large enough so the ballroom is subdivided with moveable walls (also neutral colored) that barely muffle the fantastic time being had by the group next door. (The group next to you is always having a better time...it works just like the fast lane at supermarkets.)

Speakers use the sound system provided by the conference center. The system is carefully tuned to precisely the same frequency as either the nearby airport control tower or to a neighboring radio station to maximize the interference.

All conference centers have installed the same climate control system. It has two settings...tropic or sub-arctic. It is impossible to predict which setting will be used at any given time. It is safe to assume that for most of the day, the setting will be exactly opposite of the weather outside. Dressing for this can be challenging. Layering is recommended.

STANDARD ELEMENTS

All conference centers purchase the same tables, tablecloths, and chairs. The tables and placement of chairs is precisely calibrated to allow you exactly 75% of the space you actually need to open the useless notebook and to use the miniature writing pad and cheap pencil/pen supplied by the hotel (with their logo, of course).

Padding on the stacking metal frame chairs is designed to provide comfort for approximately half of the time that you will be required to sit on them. This results in Tailbone Tingle (see *Physical Conditions*) and usually results in a higher bar tab for the hotel at the end of the day. You will notice that the chairs in the bar are much more comfortable.

STANDARD ELEMENTS

FOOD

Snacks are usually provided during breaks. They always contain massive quantities of two ingredients...sugar and caffeine. One can avoid their pitfalls---sugar coma and caffeine frenzy (see *Physical Conditions*)---by drinking the water, but that can lead to Severe Bladder Tension (see *Physical Conditions*).

Your odds of having something other than chicken to eat for entrees are roughly the same as winning the lottery. This is because the planners are playing the odds regarding foods the most people will like. It's also because the chicken is cheaper and they'll make more money on the seminar. Fortunately for you, most hotels are accustomed to the thriftiness of Seminar Planners and are fairly creative at disguising the chicken as other things.

The chicken will be served in large group settings with tables set for eight to ten people to help expand opportunities for participant interaction. See the previous section for a list of the valuable information that gets exchanged.

THE BAR

This is where the real results of the conference take place. Seasoned seminar survivors will tell you that participants and presenters alike assemble here at the end of the day (a few slip out and start early) to deaden the portion of their brain that is not already numb from the day's sessions. Before the alcohol takes effect, and sometimes afterward, the group discusses what they have been through and pools their collective knowledge on the subject at hand. This is often the most productive part of the entire seminar.

STANDARD ELEMENTS

CHARACTERS

SEMINAR COORDINATOR

This is usually a staff person from the sponsoring organization who is filled to the brim with self-importance. Their mission is to ensure the smooth operation of the seminar.

They frequently leap in front of the group to provide lengthy incomprehensible verbal instructions regarding the locations of upcoming portions of the seminar. No one ever listens to these instructions---they just ask other participants as they move, in herd fashion, toward the next location.

The coordinator is also responsible for distributing and collecting the seminar review forms, which are used to validate the opinions of seminar organizers about the success of the seminar. The coordinator is usually one of the few people in the audience to understand the seminar inside humor technique used by some speakers.

POSSIBLE SOLUTIONS

✘ Direct people to the wrong room or floor and credit the coordinator with the information.

✘ Have bogus urgent messages delivered to them just before the end of sessions.

✘ Ask them the same inane question repeatedly but with slightly altered wording. (Caution: This may thoroughly annoy fellow participants unless they are in on the joke.)

STANDARD ELEMENTS

SEMINAR PLANNER

May be the same person as the Seminar Coordinator. Could be a staff person or a volunteer from the organization sponsoring the seminar. They dedicated the last year of their life to this event and are quick to tell you so (though they prefer to hear it from someone else). The Seminar Planner provides the inspiration for a wealth of anecdotes shared by speakers, the Seminar Coordinator, and the Planner themselves, which are meaningful only to them.

POSSIBLE SOLUTIONS

✘ Avoid the Planners unless you have a burning desire to hear how this seminar has affected their life.

✘ If you are certain you will never return to another of these, pick the absolute worst aspect of the seminar and tell them how wonderful it was.

✘ Just before they announce the name(s) of other people who helped, stand up, walk to the podium, and deliver a rambling pointless acceptance speech. Then leave the room. Quickly.

STANDARD ELEMENTS

PRESENTERS

FLATLINER

Utilizes the lecture approach to present the material. Frequently the "Finance Person", this speaker selects only the most excruciatingly boring material for presentation and then delivers it with only sporadic "uhs" and "ums" to break the steady monotone string of verbiage. There will be no trace of humor in this speaker's presentation. Participants have been known to slip into comas or expire near the end of these presentations resulting in the name attributed to this speaker.

POSSIBLE SOLUTIONS

✘ Brush up on your underutilized spit balls skills

✘ Read a book

✘ Ask them pointless or sarcastic questions. They won't understand.

✘ Ask them whatever they just said---repeatedly. This will thoroughly annoy them and amuse your fellow participants when they rouse from their slumber and realize what you are doing.

STANDARD ELEMENTS

DRILL SERGEANT

This speaker uses the FOG (Fear of God) approach to retain audience attention. They move about the room delivering rapid-fire questions, which would require years of research to answer (research the speaker has already conducted), to the individual who at that precise moment is the least attentive one in the room. Seating Strategy is irrelevant in these sessions. The ABL (Absolute Boredom Level) of participants is generally extremely low during these sessions. Information retention, however, tends to be even lower because participants are so concerned about being the next question assault victim that they focus on speaker movements and Apparent Alertness Techniques instead of the material being presented. (See *Tools & Techniques* for more information on the techniques referenced here.)

STANDARD ELEMENTS

POSSIBLE SOLUTIONS

✘ Ask them lots of irrelevant questions.

✘ Snore loudly. It will infuriate the instructor and make you a hero with fellow participants.

✘ Skip the session. Who needs this stress? You'll probably learn more in the bar anyway.

STANDARD ELEMENTS

THE COMEDIAN WANNABE

These speakers fall into one of three categories: Good, Bad, or the Incredible Geek.

The Good piece together their material with jokes that participants jot down attentively. Rarely do participants remember what the presentation was about---the jokes were far better. These are quite often the most popular speakers at the Seminar.

The Bad usually recognize during their presentation that it would have been advisable to test their jokes on real people instead of the mirror. After several long quiet pauses in their presentation, they typically revert to the Flatliner approach which is more their style anyway.

The Incredible Geek laughs at their own jokes, which are filled with jargon or are seminar inside humor. They are the only person laughing (except for the Seminar Coordinator who chimes in on the inside jokes, much like Ed McMahon) This audience is irrelevant to this presentation style.

POSSIBLE SOLUTIONS

If they are good:
- ✔ Take notes

- ✔ Sit back and enjoy.

If they are bad:
- ✘ Laugh when it's not the punch line. This will really throw them off.

- ✘ Use scorecards (see *Tools & Techniques, Destroying Speaker Confidence*)

If they are Geeks:
- ✘ Leave

- ✘ Tell them afterward how funny they were

STANDARD ELEMENTS

FOG HORN

Temporary participant deafness may be caused when these speakers choose to use the microphone. No amplification would be required if these individuals were to speak from the 50-yard line of the Rose Bowl.

One must remain alert to the possibility of encountering one of these speakers. For those who do not come prepared, napkins or doughnuts from the break table may be quickly substituted for professional quality earplugs. Participants choosing this approach should consider hand positions to aid in concealing their impromptu earplugs and to make themselves appear attentive. Careful attention must be used to avoid Forehead Slumber Rash (see *Physical Conditions*).

STANDARD ELEMENTS

POSSIBLE SOLUTIONS

✖ Ask them questions so softly they can't hear. Never increase the volume.

✖ Alternate speaking loudly and softly.

✖ Visibly stuff paper, donuts or anything available into your ears.

✖ Track the flinches from audience members when the volume hits peaks. As you become more sophisticated at this you can also do an analysis of the distance from the speakers and the number of people affected.

✖ Don't bother trying to focus on anything else. The volume will make it impossible.

A Humorous Self-Help Guide

STANDARD ELEMENTS

CHURCH MOUSE

Invariably following the Fog Horn, this speaker looks directly at the podium and avoids the microphone as they whisper what they have to say. No amount of amplification would be sufficient to overcome the inaudible character of this person's speech pattern. This is true even after participants overcome the disturbing sensation of deafness and remember to remove the doughnuts from their ears. It is rumored, though, that dogs are able to hear these speakers clearly at considerable distances.

POSSIBLE SOLUTIONS

✘ Whisper back.

✘ Stare blankly as if you did not hear. This will not require acting ability.

✘ Talk with you neighbor quietly. Read a book. Play a game. Do pretty much whatever you want. The speaker will never know since they don't look up from the podium.

STANDARD ELEMENTS

MR. ACRONYM

Although encountered more frequently in technical and governmental organizations, this individual can be found in virtually every industry. Occasionally they get so wrapped up in their jargon that they cease using words and speak solely in acronyms. Twenty-minute presentations would expand to several hours if they filled in the meanings. Rarely do any participants have any idea what these speakers are saying. Fifteen minutes into the presentation, most participants are still attempting to use the seminar schedule to help them develop clues to what this speaker is talking about.

STANDARD ELEMENTS

POSSIBLE SOLUTIONS

✘ Jot down some of their acronyms. Mix and match them when you ask questions. The speaker will either be confused or spend lots of time straightening out the mess you created.

✘ Ask a follow up question mixing the acronyms again.

✘ Make up your own acronyms like IDS (Incredibly Dull Speaker) or IAU (Incomprehensible Acronym Usage). Include them in your questions and then wait for the inevitable questions. Your fellow participants will love it when you answer and may buy you drinks later. (Don't do this if you have another session with the same speaker unless you enjoy being in the hot seat.)

✘ Count the acronyms used. Count the frequency of each.

✘ Jot down the acronyms used. See how many words you can form with them. See how many variations you can come up with for pronunciation of them.

STANDARD ELEMENTS

LAST MINUTE FILL-IN

This speaker ALWAYS begins with an apology for having been called in at the last minute. Invariably, they are the third cousin of the janitor who once worked at the same complex as the world renowned authority who was to have been the speaker. With the possible exception of the Seminar Coordinator and the Seminar Groupies, none of the participants listen to anything this speaker says after that first sentence.

POSSIBLE SOLUTIONS

✘ Make up wild rumors about the absence of the original speaker. Ask the fill-in if they are true. Some possibilities are an affair with the fill-in's spouse, an espionage mission, bought off by the competitors, etc.

✘ Point out any inconsistencies between the fill-ins comments and the directory, previous comments, or work by the original speaker.

STANDARD ELEMENTS

BRAND NEW SPEAKER

Perspiring profusely, this individual wastes no time convincing the audience that their largest previous audience was the janitor who listened inattentively as they practiced the speech repeatedly the previous night. Audiences to these speakers have been known to have time to read novels while the speaker reorganized note cards that literally flew out of their shaking hands as they attempted to turn the overhead projection image right side up.

POSSIBLE SOLUTIONS

✘ Anticipate the direction of the presentation. Ask questions that jump ahead several steps.

✘ Interrupt to ask for validation of your understanding of a point made early in the speech, particularly if the whole presentation builds on that concept. State it exactly opposite of what the speaker said.

✘ Get up and leave.

STANDARD ELEMENTS

PARTICIPANTS

SEMINAR GROUPIES

These people can always be found during breaks and after the sessions clustered around the speakers. They ask intense (but usually inane) questions of those speakers hoping to separate themselves from the crowd and remain lodged in the speaker's memory for future networking possibilities. These people can usually also be found near the Seminar Coordinator hoping to get tips on other speakers and to learn the subtle nuances of Seminar Inside Humor.

STANDARD ELEMENTS

POSSIBLE SOLUTIONS

✘ Unobtrusively block their path to the speaker. Ask them inane questions to keep them occupied until the speaker departs.

✘ Tell them you are shy but would like to get an autograph from the speaker.

✘ Listen in on their questions. Later, strike up conversation and give them contradictory information that supposedly came from the speaker or coordinator.

✘ Feed them in advance some "inside" information on the speaker's unusual preferences. You'll only get to do this once, so make it count.

STANDARD ELEMENTS

KNOW-IT-ALL

This individual seeks out opportunities to discuss seminar topics in monologue fashion. "Questions" are always phrased in an appropriate manner to let other participants know that this individual knows everything there is to know about the subject and should really be the speaker and not a participant. Learn to identify this individual quickly and avoid them at all costs. They have no friends and if they latch on to you early, and you will be stuck with them for the entire seminar.

STANDARD ELEMENTS

POSSIBLE SOLUTIONS

✘ Introduce them to a friend (preferably someone you would like to become a former friend). Then spot another friend (or someone you would like to become a friend) and excuse yourself.

✘ Pretend your pager just went off and excuse yourself.

✘ Run, Dick. Run.

STANDARD ELEMENTS

CLUELESS ONE

Although markedly similar to the Know-It-All who is supremely confident of their comprehensive knowledge, the Clueless One has no idea that they know absolutely nothing about anything. They ask lots of questions without absorbing any of the answer. Invariably they are still asking questions 10 minutes after the scheduled end of the last session of the day----completely oblivious to the answers and to the growing hostility from fellow participants who have developed Tailbone Tingle and are ready to head to the hotel bar.

STANDARD ELEMENTS

POSSIBLE SOLUTIONS

✘ Deliberately feed them bogus or contradictory information, which will further confuse them.

✘ Introduce them to the Know It All. They will probably get along fabulously.

✘ Give them the wrong room number for the closing session or make sure that you are in a different session.

✘ Buy them a drink or two. These people can be great fun as you tell them extraordinarily tall tales.

STANDARD ELEMENTS

OAT SOWER

During breaks and at the bar the previous night, this person sends obvious signals that they are "available" to anyone who wants them. They may be male or female. They may be recently divorced. They almost certainly have a higher level of interest in sex and a lower standard of moral behavior than the norm.

As a female Oat Sower, her attire will be adequately outrageous to earn the disdain of the women, the fascination of the men, and, occasionally, the distraction of the speaker. She purchases perfume by the gallon.

Male Oat Sowers constantly scan everyone around them seeking female Oat Sowers. The more brash ones will weave sexual innuendoes into every conversation, monitoring responses for even the faintest glimmer of interest.

Almost everyone is fascinated by the behavior of this individual.

STANDARD ELEMENTS

POSSIBLE SOLUTIONS

✘ Buy them a drink in the name of the Hunk or the Party Animal and then introduce them.

✘ Make a note of the people with whom they are very friendly one day and don't speak the next. This information could prove lucrative.

STANDARD ELEMENTS

HUNK

With a flash of his dazzling smile and the display of his attire, which is straight out of the latest fashion magazine, this individual captivates most of the women at the seminar. He can always be found in the bar after the sessions---usually surrounded by women fascinated by his quasi-legitimate tales of pseudo adventure. He rarely contributes anything to the seminar or takes anything home from it. More important to him is the opportunity to display himself to a new crowd. Sometimes his disappearance coincides with that of the Oat Sower.

POSSIBLE SOLUTIONS

✘ Introduce him to a female Oat Sower after purchasing her a drink in his name.

✘ Compliment him on his clothes and tell him that you saw something just like it in an issue of "GQ" last year. He will probably go shopping immediately to update his wardrobe.

STANDARD ELEMENTS

PARTY ANIMAL

Rarely does this person make it to the first session each day. Occasionally, they are able to come down for lunch. After all, they were up most of the night drinking the latest trendy beverage, dancing, and carousing with the other party animals. Their absence from the session, however, is not really relevant because they are often the Marketing People who are only there to schmooze and sell their product anyway.

STANDARD ELEMENTS

POSSIBLE SOLUTIONS

✘ Find out their boss' name and leave a series of increasingly agitated messages for them with instructions to call first thing in the morning.

✘ Have them paged during the early sessions.

✘ Schedule an early wake up call for them.

✘ Tell the Hunk or the Oat Sower that the Party Animal found them very attractive. Then sit back and watch the fun.

STANDARD ELEMENTS

MISS PERKY

Due to some unknown law of nature, this is almost always a female. She was a cheerleader in high school or college and is always perky. On the third day of the seminar when everyone else is hung over from nightly drinking, bloated from eating bigger meals than normal and from taking advantage of every break time snack, Miss Perky is trying to arrange a night on the town. Never mind that she has been right with the rest of the group until the wee hours of the morning. She is always in the seminar room a half-hour before the sessions begin in the morning. Many participants will gladly contribute money to send Miss Perky home early from the seminar.

POSSIBLE SOLUTIONS

✘ **Never, never** give her any beverage or food with caffeine. All that bouncing off the walls will not be a pretty sight.

✘ Get people around her to yawn frequently.

✘ Point out the Wall Flower to Miss Perky. It will become her personal mission to improve their life.

✘ Conspire with fellow participants to keep Miss Perky away from the Seminar Coordinator. The combination of these two is dangerous and could make life miserable as the seminar progresses.

✘ Take up a collection from other participants to send Miss Perky far away. Collect a 20% management fee for coordinating this effort.

STANDARD ELEMENTS

WALL FLOWER

One has to look closely for these people. They invariably choose a seating strategy (see *Tools & Techniques*) to minimize exposure to the rest of the group. During breaks, they either slip immediately out of the room and disappear, or they never move from their chair. After each session ends, they vanish from the face of the earth and are not seen again until the next morning's session. Unless they are there because they were the only person their boss had available to send, they probably are the only ones who return with a full understanding of what was presented. Unfortunately, they miss out on the personal interaction where most of the valuable information exchange takes place at seminars.

STANDARD ELEMENTS

POSSIBLE SOLUTIONS

✘ Have them paged. It will create internal trauma like you have never seen.

✘ Position yourself so that you can inconspicuously catch their eye during the sessions. Wink at them or do things to distract them.

✘ Tell the instructor in advance that this person is an expert in the field.

✘ Arrange for an Idea Monger or Know-It-All to sit beside them so that the Wallflower is between them and the speaker. The Wallflower will be caught in an extremely uncomfortable game of tennis. Head left…"How do I get out of here? Head right…"I'm getting sick."

STANDARD ELEMENTS

IDEA MONGER

This person is infatuated with their ideas and is oblivious to the possibility that there could be another approach to the issue at hand. They present their own ideas by ramming them down everyone's throat and ridiculing any conflicting information presented by the speaker or other participants no matter how ludicrous their own concept or how logical the arguments. This is the person who will argue that the sky is not blue, that the Pope is not Catholic, and that Elvis is still alive. They thoroughly annoy both speakers and fellow participants alike, especially when they turn out to be correct.

STANDARD ELEMENTS

POSSIBLE SOLUTIONS

✘ Identify them early and find ways to prevent them from getting opportunities to gain control of the microphone.

✘ Prepare the participant microphone so that you have the ability to deliver an electric shock to the person holding it. Deliver it quickly and often when the Idea Monger gets the microphone.

✘ Have the Idea Monger paged with a bogus emergency. They'll love the attention and fellow participants will love their absence.

STANDARD ELEMENTS

PRESENTATION STYLES & METHODS

Speakers may employ a variety of presentation styles, tools, and activities in an attempt to capture the interest of their audience. Most approaches are designed to help repeat the message for reinforcement and be entertaining, though not necessarily in that order.

Speakers also have an arsenal of tools, ranging from marker boards and simple handouts to elaborate video productions. They may use these to improve the chances that their message will be retained. These tools also increase the chances of participants remaining awake to the end of the presentation.

If enough participants fail to expire AND reviews are completed with positive feedback, the speaker's chances of getting another "gig" or getting referral business increase dramatically. As a result, participants may be exposed to several of the tools described in the pages that follow. Truly desperate speakers may utilize all these tools in a single presentation. Participants are usually alert but bewildered at the conclusion of these sessions.

STANDARD ELEMENTS

In addition to the use of audio/visual tools, speakers may use a variety of presentation approaches to acquire and maintain audience interest. Their success varies depending on how closely their personality matches the style, how well the style fits with the material, and how receptive the audience is to the approach. For example, humor tends to be less than effective when presenting financial analysis information to a group of yak handlers. Of course, that combination has little chance of being dynamic no matter how effective the style.

Several styles you may encounter and ways to deal with them are described in the next few pages. Following that are descriptions of some presentation methods speakers might use.

STANDARD ELEMENTS

HUMOR

Few seminar speakers actually achieve humor, though virtually all try. Their jokes tend to fall into one of two categories: UH (Universal Humor) or SIJ (Seminar Inside Jokes). Speakers using the former usually are frequent seminar speakers and have compiled a library of jokes to fit any audience. These jokes are usually very old or so generic that they are not funny to anyone. Many participants, however, may have already turned on their auto-pilot, and chuckle as a reflex action with the unfortunate effect of reinforcing the speaker's perception that the jokes are humorous.

Seminar Inside Jokes leave Seminar Coordinators, Planners, and Groupies (and sometimes the speaker) rolling in the aisles while the rest of the audience sits attentively waiting for the punch line and wondering what is wrong with the people in the aisles.

On rare occasions, speakers actually deliver humorous material. This, rather than lecture content, is what participants remember.

STANDARD ELEMENTS

POSSIBLE SOLUTIONS

✘ If the humor is not good, learn to anticipate the joke timing. This may not be easy. Get a group of fellow participants to follow your signal and laugh together---two lines before the punch line.

✘ If the jokes are lead balloons, slip a "Dr. Kervorkian" business card in the speaker's material.

✘ Use the Joke Score Card described in the *Tools & Techniques* section.

STANDARD ELEMENTS

CLICHÉ LINK

Some speakers have assembled an impressive array of clichés which they string together to form a speech. Initially you may have a difficult time enjoying these speakers because they often force clichés to fit an awkward application in their logic path (see the *Speaker Rating Scorecard and Quantum Logic Leap* in *Tools & Techniques*). Over time, however, you will begin to find these speakers fascinating. You can keep track of the number of clichés they have used. Some of them have truly remarkable talent in this area.

POSSIBLE SOLUTIONS

✖ Write down the clichés as they are used. Jumble them. Reassemble them in a poem or story about the presenter. It will look like you are attentively taking notes. This will drive other participants nuts since they won't be hearing anything worth writing down.

✖ Score the speaker for the number of clichés used in a sentence or paragraph. Deduct points for inappropriate clichés.

1 cliché	Run of the Mill
2 clichés	Knows the Ropes
3 clichés	Most Excellent
4 clichés	Larger than Life
5 clichés	Candidate for the Cliché Hall of Fame

STANDARD ELEMENTS

STREAM OF CONSCIOUSNESS

Participants initially experience a heightened level of anxiety as they attempt to find links between what the speaker is saying and the outline, the topic, or the seminar in general. Aimless meandering from one disjointed concept to another unrelated topic make this mission impossible.

Many participants have difficulty accepting this. Instead, they assume that the speaker is communicating on some higher plane. They begin to doubt their own intellectual ability. After all, this person must be really bright and talented to have been selected as a speaker.

Eventually, almost all participants that the speaker is guiding them along a pinball-like path from Point A to Point B. They also come to realize that there really is no point after all to this exercise.

POSSIBLE SOLUTIONS

✘ Track the number of direction changes without transitions. This requires rapt attention as shifts can be quite sudden and are rarely accompanied by any change in voice pattern.

✘ Observe the quizzical look of other participants. Attempt to determine the exact time when they achieve the same enlightenment you have just experienced.

✘ Develop a list of questions that have nothing to do with anything on the agenda or with anything the speaker said. Participants who have achieved enlightenment will quickly realize that your questions are satirical. They will eagerly await the bizarre responses you are likely to get from the speaker. Participants who haven't grasped the situation will become even more bewildered.

STANDARD ELEMENTS

RHETORICAL QUESTIONS

Most often, this style involves questions being posed and answered by the speaker. Awkward but brief pauses are common in the early stages of this style presentation as participants actually attempt to answer the questions posed by the speaker. After a few tries, they realize that these are fill in the blank questions with no real blanks. At this point participants cease to make any attempt, even mentally, to answer the questions.

Less common and more disturbing to participants, is the speaker who demands specific answers and won't proceed until getting an exact match down to the pronunciation of words in the answer. In some instances, audiences who misinterpreted this style for the more common non-question have brought the presentation to a grinding halt by failing to produce any answer, let alone the "correct" one.

STANDARD ELEMENTS

POSSIBLE SOLUTIONS

✘ Respond quickly with an answer so preposterous that it stuns the speaker and audience into a prolonged awkward silence. Give no indication that you recognize how idiotic your statement was. This will make it even more difficult for the speaker to respond.

✘ Wave your hand after each question and loudly say "Ooh, ooh, ooh!" to proclaim that you know the answer---even if you don't. After your first answer, the speaker will be far too gun shy to call on you again.

STANDARD ELEMENTS

PERPETUAL PLOT

There are no surprises in this style presentation. The format is always the same: I'm going to tell you <u>fill-in-the-blank</u>...I'm telling you <u>fill-in-the-blank</u>...I told you <u>fill-in-the-blank</u>. As if this isn't bad enough, there will be total symmetry to the lecture (and lecture is the word). The singsong speech pattern will never vary. There will be an equal number of points (probably three) to each section of the speech. And any jokes will be so generic that they could (and probably will) be told to any group of people on earth with the same mirth making impact.

It probably comes as no surprise that in elementary school this speaker was a big fan of Nancy Drew or Hardy Boys novels where the plot never chang----only the names of the characters and some of the scenery.

STANDARD ELEMENTS

POSSIBLE SOLUTIONS

✘ Interrupt to ask questions about material that comes much later in the lecture. You may get lucky and have the speaker continue from that point concluding the presentation early.

✘ Near the end of the lecture, ask if they are planning to cover topics you know will not be included. Do this several times with different topics.

STANDARD ELEMENTS

QUESTIONS AT THE END

This speaker's favorite song is "I Did It My Way." They tell you up front that you are not to interrupt their speech with annoying questions so you should save them for the end. This may be because they don't have any use for alternate schools of thought, or it may be due to their lack of ability to reorient themselves to their notes if distracted in a high pressure situation like a room full of people staring at them. This is particularly common among inexperienced speakers or people covering new or unfamiliar material.

STANDARD ELEMENTS

POSSIBLE SOLUTIONS

✘ Raise your hand constantly then quickly drop it. This works best if you are on the back row.

✘ Look at them quizzically every chance you get.

STANDARD ELEMENTS

TV PRODUCTION

This presentation has been developed with painstaking detail. It almost certainly contains complex audio/visual aids requiring split second timing. It is usually combined with a speaker whose ability to ad lib ranks right up there with deer caught in headlights. This speaker constantly watches the clock and can break out in a cold sweat if any "scene" takes more (or even worse, less) time than allotted in the storyboard.

When the actual time to complete a scene dramatically exceeds the planned time, these speakers have been known to skip scenes to remain on schedule (see *Tools & Techniques*, *Quantum Logic Leap*) because they see success in terms of the schedule rather than the content. In rare instances, these speakers recognize the audience confusion created when they have leapt forward. Their anxiety is compounded when they backtrack to fill in the missing information. While this helps the audience, it may cause coronary disturbances for the speaker.

You should never vacation with these people, as they will make the experience a trip into Hell.

POSSIBLE SOLUTIONS

✘ Deliberately interrupt to ask questions that you know will prolong a segment of the presentation. If they manage to get the presentation back on track, ask a follow up question on something previously covered.

✘ Frown regularly even if you clearly understand what they are saying. They may extend explanations and begin to perspire profusely as their schedule goes further awry.

STANDARD ELEMENTS

HANDOUTS

The **Sketchy Outline** is used by the complete novice and by the consummate seminar speaker. Novices prepare the outline quickly during the first draft of their presentation. Then they rehearse and modify until the presentation bears little resemblance to the outline. Participants in these sessions are absorbed by the effort to reconcile the outline to the speech. Frustration eventually gives way to Cerebral Relocation (see *Physical Conditions*).

Consummate seminar performers have given the speech many times before and have refined their outline each time so that it closely parallels the flow of discussion. Participants can easily follow the outline and record notes properly.

The **Comprehensive Handout** is prepared by speakers with a sincere desire to provide participants all of the information that the speaker has painstakingly gathered. Unfortunately, this handout makes the speaker's presentation redundant. Audiences see immediately that everything they need is in the handout. So they spend the session time punching holes in the thick document using their free cheap pen with the hotel logo so they can add it to their useless binder.

STANDARD ELEMENTS

POSSIBLE SOLUTIONS

✘ Replace the stack of handouts with your own (which you prepared in advance) as you pass it to the next person. Yours should initially include some typical key points that might go with the topic. Then it should stray wildly to extraneous topics and concepts. If possible, include several different versions to maximize the resulting confusion as participants ask questions about the contrast between the speaker's comments and the handouts.

✘ Insert a love letter ostensibly from an anonymous seminar participant to the speaker (or vice versa) as you pass the stack. It will stimulate much discussion during the remainder of the seminar.

✘ Insert Free Drink coupons (present at the bar---courtesy of the speaker).

STANDARD ELEMENTS

CHARTS AND GRAPHS

Some speakers include incomprehensible charts or graphs in their presentations. These represent years of in-depth analysis of a once simple and straightforward theory. These charts generally involve lots of intersecting circles, arrows, and/or other geometric shapes with descriptive labels placed all over them. You could spend years attempting to achieve the "enlightenment" these charts have brought the speaker.

The chart has a better use, however. Carefully grasp the paper on which the chart is printed in the lower right corner. Now flip the paper over and either trace the chart on the back of the paper or apply some of the doodling techniques described in the Alertness Simulation section of the chapter on *Tools & Techniques*.

POSSIBLE SOLUTIONS

✘ Challenge the basic concept underlying the entire research project. Use lots of big words and sound confident and authoritative even if your argument makes no sense. Fellow participants will assume that they have not fully grasped the concept---and they probably never will.

✘ Question the accuracy of the scale in the chart.

✘ Ask if the study has been validated through repetition by other researchers. Introduce contradictory evidence from fictitious researchers.

STANDARD ELEMENTS

EASELS AND MAGIC MARKERS

This is a low-tech version of the overhead transparency and slides. It is typically used as a large static presentation of an outline to guide the lecture (or discussion). Participants often refer to the printed version they received in their useless binder because they cannot read the version at the front of the room despite hours of artful preparation by the speaker.

This method is perfect for capturing ideas generated during audience participation sessions (see Audience Participation later in this chapter). This approach allows maximum flexibility in the presentation path. While conceptually excellent, the effectiveness of this approach is usually offset by the inability of the speaker (or able assistant) to spell correctly or write legibly. Consequently, participants spend more time attempting to determine the correlation between what was just said and what was written than on the continued discussion.

STANDARD ELEMENTS

POSSIBLE SOLUTIONS

✘ Argue vehemently over the accuracy and appropriateness of subtle nuances in the words chosen to express the concepts presented by fellow participants.

✘ Frequently correct the spelling of words used on the board.

✘ Toss out absurd word associations attempting to take the audience on a tangent to the topic at hand. Not only will this provide a good opportunity for the speaker to demonstrate his skill at keeping the discussion on track, but it will also provide conversation starters at the bar (i.e. "Were you in the session with the fruit loop who said..."). This is not a good strategy, however, if your boss or a co-worker is attending the seminar.

✘ Volunteer to write for the speaker. Blatantly misspell words to divert the focus of fellow participants.

STANDARD ELEMENTS

OVERHEADS

Used effectively, overheads allow the instructor to take static information which would have been excruciatingly dull on paper and make it large. Some speakers simply photocopy their typed page onto transparencies. Placing the projector in Cleveland for a seminar in Atlanta would still not result in an image large enough to be read. These are the same presenters who place the transparency on the projector upside down. They are oblivious to the audience members twisting in their seats and squinting their eyes until one of the participants points out the *faux pas* to the speaker (see *Tools & Techniques, Destroying Speaker Confidence*).

More experienced speakers have spent outrageous sums of money to have their transparencies professionally typeset in color hoping that the introduction of color will stave off the climbing ABL (see *Tools & Techniques*) for a few more minutes. Truly excellent overhead aficionados use grease pencils or markers to simulate animation by actually altering or adding to their expensive color typeset overhead transparencies. If performed successfully, they can transform excruciatingly dull information into the truly mundane.

STANDARD ELEMENTS

POSSIBLE SOLUTIONS

✘ Take your own laser pointer. Point to items on the screen which in no way, shape or form, correspond to the speaker's comments.

✘ Get someone to slip in before the presentation in a hotel uniform and either shuffle or replace the speaker's overheads.

STANDARD ELEMENTS

SLIDES

The next step up the presentation evolutionary chain is the slide show. Here the presenter can combine their lecture with a dark room and large static color slides to send the audience into deep sleep in record time. Though many slides are simply revisions of the color transparency approach, this medium allows the introduction of actual photography and music.

With multiple projectors, simple animation can be created to dazzle the poor soul who spent untold hours creating it and to completely bore the audience that sees fantastic animation on TV every day. Whether the presenter uses one projector with a remote control or 32 projectors controlled by a computer, the audience will remember the one slide that was in upside down long after they have forgotten the message in the show.

STANDARD ELEMENTS

POSSIBLE SOLUTIONS

✘ Replace the slides with more interesting images, preferably something that might prove embarrassing (but not illegal) to the presenter.

✘ Bring your own remote control for the slide projector. Change the slides backwards and forwards at random. Move the slides twice in the opposite direction that the speaker attempts to move them.

✘ If the slide projector(s) is (are) tied to audio tape with synchronized cues, then unplug one or more projectors midway through the presentation or wave a powerful magnet near the tape.

STANDARD ELEMENTS

COMPUTER PRESENTATIONS

Thanks to the miracle of technology, many excruciatingly dull slide shows have been recreated with sizzling new effects like fades, dissolves and drop in text. This transforms dull material into dull material with pizzazz.

Widely available software now allows presenters to develop presentations directly on the computer without expensive graphic designers, slide creation, and cumbersome truckloads of audio-visual equipment. This means that dynamic, charismatic speakers can apply their talents to their audio-visual presentation. It also means that the Finance Person and the Flatliner can do the same.

Finally, the new technology allows the designer wannabes to take that sharp image from their monitor, send it through a projector and convert it into an excellent demonstration of Pointalism. Suerat is probably turning in his grave.

STANDARD ELEMENTS

POSSIBLE SOLUTIONS

✘ Loosen a cable connection between the computer and the projector.

✘ If seated near the computer during the presentation, inconspicuously tap the space bar or arrow keys when the speaker isn't looking.

✘ Check the computer file directory for draft versions of the presentation. Open the earliest version instead of the final one. If there is one with a humorous name, open it instead.

✘ Use a laser pointer to point at the walls and/or ceiling to distract the audience.

STANDARD ELEMENTS

VIDEOS

Videos are the top of the audio/visual food chain. Most seminars include at least one video done by pros (low budget events may have amateur videos). Low budget seminars use a single TV clearly visible only to the people in the center of the first rows. People who can see the TV experience temporary deafness from the volume required for people in the back to grasp the video concept.

Regardless of the production budget and attention given to the audience's ability to see the image, no speaker ever knows how to properly operate the TV-VCR combination and no tape ever begins at precisely the program start. The audience watches and listens to static or watches the speaker (and the volunteer who helped them start the TV and VCR) reset it to the beginning. Once the video begins, the audience (now with ringing in their ears from the static blast) is asked if the volume is OK. The stunned silent stares are interpreted as "yes", and the volume is left at full.

Truly good videos establish the contrast needed to demonstrate just how bad the speaker really is. Truly bad videos can be even more entertaining than the good ones.

STANDARD ELEMENTS

POSSIBLE SOLUTIONS

✘ Switch the tapes. Substitute some classic film like "Plan 9 from Outer Space."

✘ Casually press the Fast Forward button on the VCR before the session starts.

✘ Disconnect the cable leading from the VCR to the TV. The speaker and assistant will be so absorbed with checking for Channel 3 that they'll never think to check this.

✘ Bring a universal remote with you. Program it for the brand of VCR used. Start and stop the VCR at random times throughout the presentation.

STANDARD ELEMENTS

STUPID NAME GAME

Smaller sessions with available time almost always begin with some variation of the stupid name game to help participants bond so they will participate. These games always involve going around the room one person at a time so that everyone can learn a little something about everyone else. Virtually all participants hate these games; however, you can add a little spice to the game by tossing in something like "My name is <u>insert your name here</u> and I like to select random participants in these sessions and kill them when they say something stupid." From that point on, no one will remember anyone else's name and everyone will be concentrating on having something brilliant to say when it is their turn.

STANDARD ELEMENTS

POSSIBLE SOLUTIONS

✘ Use a bogus name. Pick something believable like Beth Jones or a celebrity name like Cheryl Tiegs. The first approach will create more long term confusion and the second will usually result in immediate gratification.

✘ Introduce yourself using the name of the person next to you. Get them to reciprocate. Then switch regularly throughout the seminar.

A Humorous Self-Help Guide

STANDARD ELEMENTS

AUDIENCE INVOLVEMENT

Almost always follows a Stupid Name Game in small sessions. This approach may also be used in large sessions. It requires alertness and is largely unpopular except among Seminar Groupies, Know-It-Alls, and Idea Mongers (see *Characters*).

Except at a conference on extroversion, this approach tends to be counterproductive because participants focus exclusively on whether they might have to speak, how they can avoid it, and what they will say to avoid sounding stupid if their avoidance techniques are unsuccessful. They also worry about speaking in run on sentences like the previous one.

In some cases, this approach can be thwarted by responding to questions with questions (see *Tools & Techniques, Destroying Speaker Confidence, Debilitating Questions*).

STANDARD ELEMENTS

POSSIBLE SOLUTIONS

✘ Inject answers or questions so ludicrous or disjointed that no one will ask again.

✘ Filibuster. Ask a question that never ends. This requires good breathing ability to avoid interruption.

✘ Burst out in diabolical laughter at inappropriate times.

✘ Stare intently at a certain spot behind the speaker.

✘ Take control of the discussion. Don't let go.

STANDARD ELEMENTS

GROUP PROJECTS

By splitting the large group into smaller groups—each with an assignment—seminar coordinators and presenters hope to maximize the overall exchange of ideas. Groups may be assembled through some prearranged number/letter/color on your useless notebook or nametag, by the area in which you are seated or by the call-it-out-let's-hear-you-now group selection method (one, two, three, one, two, three...).

Regardless of the selection method, the rest of your group will either be all doctoral candidates with the subject (which is new to you) as their thesis or all imbeciles who do not even understand the topic much less solutions to the problem at hand.

NEVER volunteer to be the leader of the group because you will have to present your group's ideas to the large group when it reconvenes. If paired with the doctoral students, your responses will be beyond the speaker's comprehension and follow-up questions will be challenging to say the least. As the leader of "those with the vacant look in their eyes," your presentation will likely be met with the same looks you might get if you had just disembarked from your alien spaceship.

POSSIBLE SOLUTIONS

✘ Present something completely unrelated to the project. Your group will wonder what medication you are taking. The large group won't notice because they will be focused on their own presentation or relieved that theirs is over.

✘ Try to get in a group with Miss Perky since she will do all the work or with an Idea Monger or Know-It-All since they will gladly volunteer to be in charge.

STANDARD ELEMENTS

PANEL OF EXPERTS

Here a collection of experts has been assembled to answer participant questions about the subject at hand. Generally, they all hold similar opinions about the subject. Occasionally you will encounter a panel with diametrically opposite outlooks on the situation. This situation presents you with an opportunity to make the session vastly more interesting.

Once you have identified the difference of opinion, you should ask questions designed to exploit that difference. Success in stimulating a verbal barrage between the two panel members will not only wake your fellow participants, it will earn you their respect. If you can draw the panel members into an enraged physical brawl, you need not worry about having to buy drinks in the bar that night.

POSSIBLE SOLUTIONS

✖ Sit back and relax. The experts are probably charter members of the Mutual Admiration Society for People in Love with the Sound of Their Own Voice. You may learn something, but it's more likely that you will hear the experts compliment each other on their collective wisdom.

Surviving Seminars:

PHYSICAL CONDITIONS

"I think I'm gonna be sick."

A Humorous Self-Help Guide

PHYSICAL CONDITIONS

SEVERE BLADDER TENSION (SBT)

Increased beverage consumption, combined with reduced restroom visit frequency, brings on this condition which impairs concentration and data retention. Studies have broken the condition into three stages. Left untreated, it can create a memorable event for other participants causing permanent psychological scars for the victim.

   I.   Victim experiences mild pressure and may reposition themselves frequently in a futile attempt to temporarily relieve the building pressure.

   II. Concentration now difficult for the victim who constantly writhes in their chair. Patient regrets beverage consumption and choice of a non-elastic waistband.

   III. Victim's eyes are now bulging and explosion is imminent. Concentration is now intense but focused solely on rehearsing the route from the session to the restroom.

Treatment varies from simple preventative measures like drinking less and visiting the restroom more often, to wearing more absorbent undergarments. In a few rare cases, catheters have been installed to allow patients not to miss any of the seminar sessions.

PHYSICAL CONDITIONS

SUGAR COMA

    Brought on by the consumption of sugar laden snacks provided during breaks and unbelievably rich deserts provided with lunch, this condition causes severe drowsiness and compounds the effect of Tabletop Gravitation. It can be partially offset by consuming massive quantities of caffeine. This strategy may result in Caffeine Frenzy and will cause an upward shift of at least one level in SBT. Rarely does anyone fully counteract this condition during the seminar. It usually takes a week or more after the seminar of consuming a normal diet before the victim returns to normal.

PHYSICAL CONDITIONS

CAFFIENE FRENZY

Caused by inordinate consumption of coffee or tea (usually to counteract Sugar Coma, Eyelid Droop, or Terminal Boredom). This condition is usually characterized by incessant tapping (fingers, pencil/pen, and/or toes). If encountered early in the seminar it tends to become chronic because virtually all victims either stay up all night as a result or drink heavily to avoid staying up all night. In either case, the victim OD's on caffeine again the next day to overcome the effects of loss of sleep or hangover. Wise participants take advantage of this condition to accomplish weeks of work in compressed time.

When this condition is encountered in personalities like Miss Perky, it may be highly amusing. The amusement is quickly followed by intense irritation when they don't slow down.

Drink lots of fluids to counteract, but don't stray far from the restrooms.

PHYSICAL CONDITIONS

HANGOVER

Results from the burning desire of the participant to remain at the bar after the sessions to take advantage of the real idea exchange. Unfortunately, perceived wisdom and idea exchange tends to be directly proportional to alcohol consumption. The barroom scholars tend to be clustered around the coffee urn at the beginning of the second day's sessions while the hunk, who bought the drinks, slumbers peacefully in his room.

Everybody and their mother has a cure for this. Pick the one that works for you, but it's probably best if you don't share the need for it with your mother.

PHYSICAL CONDITIONS

TERMINAL BOREDOM

Found most often in Flatliners, Know-It-Alls, and Wall Flowers, this condition results from excessive seminar attendance, or under-stimulation, or over-stimulation. The victim has achieved a heightened state of boredom, which may be described as being jaded. They are impressed by absolutely nothing. If Elvis appeared to lead the session, this person would claim to have seen something more remarkable the previous week.

There is no known cure for this so it's best to have some fun with this person, at their expense, of course. Tell them outrageous lies so that they can claim to have already done or seen something bigger. Better yet, tell a progression of contradictory lies and get them to top each one. Award yourself points for each flip-flop.

PHYSICAL CONDITIONS

RESTRAINT DEFICIENCY

Characterized by excessive food, alcohol consumption, excessive spending, and sometimes by wild sex with other participants (or speakers, or hotel staff, or strangers off the street), this condition occurs to some degree in all but the most seasoned seminar participants. It results from the sudden freedom of being placed in a new environment with a group of strangers that will probably never be seen again. It usually results in some or all of the other physical conditions described here.

Participants with cameras can often effect immediate cures for Restraint Deficiency or generate future income possibilities from the incurable.

PHYSICAL CONDITIONS

FOREHEAD SLUMBER RASH (FSR)

Generally occurs at the end of the day. It is evidenced by red marks on the face caused by hands bracing the head to offset Tabletop Gravitation. In severe cases, the red marks may also show the texture of the tablecloth, notebook, and pencils/pens on which the victims head came to rest when they lost the battle against Tabletop Gravitation. This is a temporary condition, which invariably draws muffled snickers from fellow participants during breaks.

Pillows have been known to prevent this temporary rash but are somewhat bulky and generally frowned upon. An alternate technique involves the use of table napkins for padding atop the useless binder which is propped under the chin. Another approach is the intentional placement of objects to create patterns accompanied by claims that the rash is a new temporary tattoo craze.

PHYSICAL CONDITIONS

EYELID DROOP

Often accompanies Sugar Coma, Hangover, and/or Terminal Boredom. Affected by Tabletop Gravitation and encountered most often in early morning, late afternoon and just after lunch. If not caught early and counteracted with the antidote (caffeine) or with prosthetics (toothpicks), this condition can result in FSR. In severe cases, bruising and dental damage may result as the chin impacts the tabletop.

Increased nose altitude can cosmetically address this condition by creating the appearance that eyes are fully open. Caution is urged not to permit the mouth to gape or to permit snoring.

Recent developments have included the prescription of eyebrow pushups. These have the potential side effect of increased attention from the uninformed speaker who misinterprets the pushups as questions.

Another solution is to sketch wide open eyes, cut them out, and affix them to the outside of drooping eyelids.

PHYSICAL CONDITIONS

TAILBONE TINGLE (TT)

Evidenced by a tingling sensation near the tailbone. TT results from sitting too long on stackable metal frame conference chairs with standard inadequate padding. Left untreated, the sensation will be replaced by total numbness and possible permanent paralysis. Once it has occurred, this condition tends to reoccur with increasing frequency.

Chair padding can be supplemented to reduce the occurrence of TT. Stationary buttock aerobics may also be used but could alarm nearby participants as they strain to hear the music that caused you to dance.

Another approach with decided entertainment value is to leap from your seat as if your neighbor did something highly offensive to you. If the instructor is a Church Mouse, you can get up and do jumping jacks without them knowing.

PHYSICAL CONDITIONS

CEREBRAL RELOCATION (CR)

More commonly known by the slang term "day dreaming." Like most other seminar afflictions, this condition is brought on by boredom and is intensified by Sugar Coma and Caffeine Frenzy. Virtually all seminar participants experience this condition. Periods of CR may last from a few minutes to a few hours. In extreme cases, CR conditions may last for days or weeks. During CR periods the victim's attention wanders from the important subject matter to topics with temporarily higher priorities---vacations, to do lists, the Hunk or the Oat Sower in the group.

Treatment of CR falls into two camps---avoid it or embrace it. Followers of the first theory advocate techniques to focus thought, like counting the number of fellow participants who have slipped into CR and then rating the speaker based on the number of people and the speed at which they were driven there. Embracers recognize the rarity of quality time like this at home and seek to maximize the experience. They come prepared with notes to channel their CR time down personally rewarding paths. An alternate but less productive approach is to speculate on the destination to which fellow participants have cerebrally relocated.

Surviving Seminars:

TOOLS & TECHNIQUES

"If I had a hammer, I'd hit myself in the head with it…"

TOOLS & TECHNIQUES

SEATING STRATEGY

Your seminar experience can vary tremendously based on where you sit. Most large seminars are set up in a lecture style layout. There is a podium and/or stage at the front of the room and rows of slightly too narrow tables carefully placed slightly too close together. This design is based on years of government sponsored research on mitigating premature boredom related migration.

The seating design, coupled with breaks that are slightly too short, provide aerobic exercise for participants moving between sessions. The inter-session movement concept was developed by seminar planners to reduce snoring related interruptions for afternoon speakers. In a serendipitous development, the plan accomplished the desired results but turned breaks into a full contact sport. Participants now clamor to get in line for the slightly too few restroom stalls or slightly too few courtesy phones. Increased blood pressure causes alertness for those participants who make it to the next session on time, though their attention is focused on the things they weren't able to do during the break. Their attention is further diverted as the participants who did accomplish break time objectives enter the session late.

TOOLS & TECHNIQUES

Regardless whether your objective is to get visibility with the speaker, disappear into the woodwork, or finish that past due assignment, it can be accomplished by careful seat location selection. Your decision can help you predict with an amazing degree of accuracy who will be sitting near you. Getting the right seat may mean giving up that restroom visit during break. A one-stage increase in Severe Bladder Tension may result (see *Physical Conditions*).

The following descriptions may prove helpful as you determine where to sit (or they may not, but they're here for your use anyway):

- FRONT ROW – These seats are usually occupied by Seminar Groupies and Organizers who want to be visible or positioned well to pop up with announcements, by Idea Mongers eager to further their cause, and by late arrivals who had successful break experiences. It's the best place to be if you have questions, want the speaker to see you, or if you want to be able to read anything the speaker projects on the giant screen.

- BACK ROW – Here you may find Oat Sowers who want a clear view of everyone in the room (they sometimes sit in the front, however, so that everyone can have a clear view of

TOOLS & TECHNIQUES

- them), Wall Flowers who don't want to be seen at all, early arrivals who bypassed the restroom to stake their claim, and the Southern Baptists who are just used to sitting there. These are the best seats in the house if you want to work on something else, if you want to complete the Speaker Rating Scorecard (see *Tools & Techniques*), if you want to visit the restroom without the crowd, or if you just want to slip out.

- SIDES – These are also good seats for those who want to slip out, for those with mild cases of claustrophobia, and for observing the crowd (toward the rear of the room). Wall Flowers may be found here along with Oat Sowers. Hunks may also sit here but usually toward the front of the room. Know-it-Alls sometimes sit here so that they can see enlightenment wash over the crowd when they speak (at least that's what they see!).

- CENTER – The middle of the room is also filled with late arrivals and is a melting pot of personalities. If you thrive on variety, this is the place to be. There are a few types of people you are almost guaranteed to meet here. Clueless Ones, who have not yet realized perimeter seats reduce climbing effort, will be in the center. So will people wearing bifocals who only want to bend their necks one way as they squint in a futile effort to read the projected image at the front. People with excellent bladder control will be here.

TOOLS & TECHNIQUES

These strategies may be completely invalid if the seminar organizers have organized the seating in one of several other formats, which are described below:

SEMI-CIRCLE – Some of the same rules apply to this set-up, but the safety net provided by tables is usually removed. This is partially offset by improved mobility but the loss of writing surface (even though it was slightly too small), and the increased visibility of lower body parts is disconcerting to most participants (except for Oat Sowers).

SQUARE – Participants are organized at tables in a square. This seating arrangement facilitates open discussion if the participants know each other or don't mind presenting their thoughts for ridicule to a group of total strangers. Know-it-alls, Idea Mongers, and Seminar Groupies LOVE this setup. Wall Flowers will be certain that they chose the wrong door and descended directly into Hell. Squares are sometimes paired with a Drill Sergeant in the middle whirling to challenge novice participants with rapidly ascending blood pressure.

TOOLS & TECHNIQUES

CIRCLE – Unless you really enjoy lots of eye contact with a group of other uncomfortable people, this will not be a fun session. Some people have been known to brace their arms and legs firmly against the doorframe as they enter these sessions. This temporarily prevents entry by others who push aggressively to remove them until the blockage is gone and they see their mistake. Others turn and bolt like cows suddenly realizing the line is not for food.

Unfortunately, the increased visibility in these sessions can also increase group awareness of individual participant absence. So you might want to practice stimulation of your gag reflex. Though it might be embarrassing to barf in a nice hotel in front of your fellow participants, it will give you a plausible reason for missing the session. It will also cause others to get sick and they'll thank you later.

CLOTHING STRATEGY

The most difficult hurdle to overcome in garment planning is acceptance that seminar weather prediction is not possible. Temperatures inside will likely be completely opposite of those outside and conditions may be radically different from one session to the next. Dramatic temperature changes have been known to occur even during a single session. These shifts are usually caused by shifts in the level of whining between hot and cold natured participants.

To cope with cold temperatures, some participants arrive bundled in enough insulated clothing to restrict movement of their extremities. This can also help prevent Tailbone Tingle but can prove disastrous during advanced stages of Severe Bladder Tension. Seasoned seminar survivors say that adventurous but cold and frustrated participants once built a fire using pages from their useless binders for fuel, rubbing cheap hotel pens together to ignite it. Open flames, however, are generally frowned upon at seminars because they tend to distract the speakers.

TOOLS & TECHNIQUES

Once the noise from chattering teeth reaches 24.5 decibels, hotel staff will shift the air conditioning system from arctic to its other setting---tropic. Almost immediately, participants begin to molt. Those who planned ahead are able to gradually shed layers. The Eskimos who prepared only for the cold notice that their clothing is reducing bladder tension by reducing the excess moisture that had accumulated in their bodies.

With few exceptions, public nudity during seminar sessions is frowned upon and so eventually the shedding of clothes reaches critical mass. At that point, the volume of sighs and whimpering blend with the rustling of pages from the useless binder in the dry air. As the volume exceeds that of the speaker, hotel staff begins the cycle again.

The only way to cope with this compressed seasonal cycle is to dress in layers.

ALERTNESS SIMULATION

You can create the appearance of taking notes and paying attention while simultaneously venturing into other dimensions by trying some of the following:

✘ Do Boredom Avoidance Exercises like creating lists of things to do and Top 10 lists of things like adjectives to describe the session or speaker, or words and phrases that really aren't but that the speaker keeps using, or reasons not to be there.

✘ Develop your Doodling Techniques by sketching common objects like your water glass, the useless binder, or the plastic chandelier. Then sketch them from different perspectives like your water glass from the chandelier. Or sketch a chandelier made of water glasses.

✘ Look straight at the incredibly boring speaker. Visualize them standing in their underwear or wearing a clown suit. Keeping a straight face is another matter.

TOOLS & TECHNIQUES

DESTROYING SPEAKER CONFIDENCE

In every seminar there is at least one speaker whose sense of rightness and arrogance infuriates audience members who know the speaker is a blustery bag of hot air. Fortunately, beneath the supremely confident surface of even the best speaker lurks at least a kernel of self-doubt. With a little effort, that kernel can be fertilized and made to grow. It is possible to take the wind out even the biggest blowhard's sails.

To be sporting, you should save these techniques for the experienced speaker described above. Using them on a Church Mouse, a Last Minute Fill-In, or a Brand New Speaker would be like shooting fish in a barrel. It's too easy to be fun. The only downside to this restriction is that experienced speakers have dealt with hecklers before so you have to beware of counterattacks. Remember that they have both the floor and the microphone.

TOOLS & TECHNIQUES

Dead Horse Indicator - Cut out the horse shown here. Attach it (glue, tape, or staple), right side up, to the back of the tent card that you wrote your name on and placed on the table in front of you.

When a particular subject has been beaten to death, flip the tent card so that your name is face down on the table. The horse, now upside down, will be facing the speaker letting them know it's time to move on.

Feel free to copy this page and distribute it to fellow participants. That way you can avoid the awkward position of being the only person watching for the topic to pass down that light filled tunnel.

A Humorous Self-Help Guide

TOOLS & TECHNIQUES

Debilitating Questions - Distraction is one of the keys to speaker demoralization. So use some of the following approaches to questions to deflect the speakers attention from their intended path.

✘ Ask about a point the speaker just made. Do this repeatedly.

✘ Ask questions that have absolutely nothing to do with the topic.

✘ Use multi-part questions that are actually five or six separate questions.

✘ Ask about points that you anticipate will come later in the presentation.

✘ Ask questions at the mid-way point or later that make it clear you failed to grasp the initial concept upon which the whole presentation is based.

✘ Inject questions so ridiculously worded that no one has any clue what you are asking. Clarify with an equally ludicrous rewording that completely changes the meaning of the initial question.

TOOLS & TECHNIQUES

✖ Filibuster. Ask a question that never ends.

✖ Present a vehemently argumentative question over subtle nuances in the concept.

✖ Immediately point out any inconsistencies in what the speaker says.

✖ Mix and match acronyms incorrectly in a lengthy question.

✖ Raise your hand and then quickly drop it----repeatedly.

✖ Look quizzically at the speaker every time they establish eye contact.

✖ Wave your hand regularly and loudly say "Ooh, ooh, ooh" as if you have something important to say. In the unlikely event the speaker calls on you, ask some inane question.

✖ Speak so softly that the person next to you can't hear clearly. The speaker will have no choice but to pretend you didn't speak or to come down into the audience.

TOOLS & TECHNIQUES

UH Factor Display Cards - Use a sheet of paper from your useless binder to record the number of "uhs" uttered by the speaker in a period of time (see the page on the UH Factor later in this section). Hold it up so the speaker can improve their performance in the next period. (They almost never do.)

An alternate approach again involves a sheet of paper from the useless binder. Write "UH" on the blank side of the page in as bold and as large letters as you can fit on the page. Each time the speaker says "uh", hold up your card. The debilitating effect of this second approach increases dramatically as more audience members hold up signs. With enough participation and a little practice, a wave effect can be created with the signs further increasing their impact.

Score Cards for Jokes - Similar to the UH Factor Scorecard, the idea is to rate the speaker's jokes. Use a scale of 1 to 10. You will probably never use the higher scores since you will be too busy writing those jokes down. Get fellow participants to do the same. This is particularly humiliating for jokes that elicit no laughter. Knowing when to hold up the score in this case may be challenging, however, (see *Humor* in *Standard Elements* for more techniques for dealing with bad humor).

SPEAKER RATING SCORECARD (SRS)

The SRS, which appears on the next page, is actually a collection of insightful measurements of a speaker's performance and impact on the audience. These measures are based on exhausting (not to be confused with exhaustive) scientific research conducted and validated over two decades. This was done in seminar sessions which seemed to last the full two decades individually. Number Two pencils should be used to complete the scorecard and calculators are permitted provided the buttons don't make noise. Believe it or not, interaction with participants around you is actually encouraged for this test.

Each individual performance measurement is described in detail in the pages following the scorecard. If you don't fully grasp the concept, that's OK. Just use your understanding to create a variation to the measure and send it in for possible inclusion in the next edition of this book. Be sure to include your name in the title of your new measurement so that all your friends will know whom to thank when they attend their next seminar.

Feel free to duplicate the SRS so that you can evaluate multiple speakers. You may also replace the seminar evaluation form with this one---it will probably be more useful.

TOOLS & TECHNIQUES

SPEAKER RATING SCORECARD

SPEAKER:
SESSION TOPIC:

CATEGORY	SCORE
Charisma Barometer Reading	
Egometer Reading	
Rate of Speech (ROS)	
UH Factor	
Visual Aid Usage Score	
Average Boredom Level (ABL)	
Table Top Gravitation Shifts	
QL2 Score	
Dead Horse Factor	
Topic Excitement Score	
TOTAL	

Surviving Seminars:

TOOLS & TECHNIQUES

SCORE	WHAT IT MEANS
800 +	Too good to be true. You are either a Seminar Groupie or the menu at your seminar included hallucinogenic substances.
600-799	Exceptional speaker. You have a strong chance of attending the next seminar as an Alumnus to tell everyone how good this one was.
400-599	Good to very good speaker. You learned something besides scorekeeping and can return from the seminar with enough new material to annoy coworkers. If properly applied, you have a good chance of securing attendance at another seminar—and you would want to go.
200-399	Ineffective Speaker. You developed scorekeeping skills and finished a variety of tasks with minimal interruptions from the speaker. Fortunately, the useless binder contained a few morsels of information for you to take home.
0-200	Not only was the speaker so bad that you can't remember what they covered (partly because you left early), but the materials in the binder and handouts truly are useless. Your seminar career is over unless your creative writing skills are exceptional.
<0	So bad that you want to write a sequel to *Surviving Seminars*.

TOOLS & TECHNIQUES

CHARISMA BAROMETER

This is a measure of the speaker's personality only. Careful measurement is required since false negative readings are possible if there are intense reactions to other factors such as the topic, the presentation style, or the room temperature.

Use the free pencil or pen with the hotel logo to fill this barometer to the appropriate level for the speaker in question. (Pencil is advised as speakers often give falsely high ratings early in their presentations. Much like a real barometer with an approaching storm, the level can drop precipitously.)

At the end of the session, evaluate the entire presentation to determine the overall Charismetric Pressure. Record the score on the Speaker Scorecard.

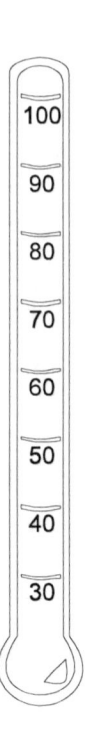

TOOLS & TECHNIQUES

EGOMETER

Self-confidence is critical to effective speaking. Unfortunately, some speakers base their level of importance on the adoration of seminar groupies. Then their heads inflate. Their mouths serve as pressure relief valves but are not always effective at regulating rapid pressure increases. In extreme but rare cases, the speaker rises from the ground. Fortunately, they are able to grasp the microphone stand to keep them near their audience and away from the giant plastic chandeliers. Use the descriptions below to categorize your speaker and the Egometer (e gom uh tur) to determine the correct score for the Speaker Rating Scorecard.

A   Never looks audience in the eye. Babbles.
B   Knows material but lacks confidence to maintain positions when challenged.
C   Confident, knowledgeable, and effective speaker.
D   Thoroughly knowledgeable and slips subtle verbal barbs at other experts into the presentation
E   Blatantly belittles everyone. Believes their own press releases and their seminar biographies.

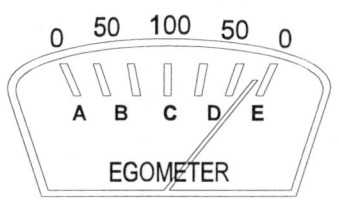

A Humorous Self-Help Guide

TOOLS & TECHNIQUES

RATE OF SPEECH (ROS)

Measured in words per minute, the ROS impacts Average Boredom Level and Tabletop Gravitation. Ideal Rates of Speech (IRS) vary, so you will need to customize this table to fit yours. Pick a speaker who talks at the pace you like. Get the person next to you to help time exactly one minute while you count the number of words spoken by the speaker. (Don't worry about disturbing your neighbor. They weren't listening anyway and will be fascinated with the scientific research you are conducting.) Insert this figure into the IRS box in the middle of the table. Now add 5 to that number for each successive column below the ideal (and subtract 5 for each successive row above). You have now developed the highly precise (insert your name here) ROS Table.

Now all you have to do is repeat the timing/word count exercise for other speakers to determine their score. Once again, you will need the help of your neighbor who by now will be honored to have been named Research Assistant to (insert your name here), Ph.D., world renowned, Speech Researchologist. (Feel free to share the other measurement tools in this book at that point...your neighbor will be awestruck, and your adopting a foreign accent will intensify this effect.)

TOOLS & TECHNIQUES

Rates of Speech that are significantly faster than your ideal can lead to Cerebral Relocation (see *Physical Conditions*) and speculation about the speaker's abuse of performance enhancing drugs. Rates significantly slower can lead to a burning desire to leap from your seat, rush to the front of the audience and forcibly extract the next words from the throat of the speaker. (No matter how tempting, this approach should be avoided.)

Use the table to determine the appropriate score decrease for a speaker's tendency to stray from your ideal. You statisticians will no doubt observe the perfect bell curve formed by the possible scores. Actual scores, however, tend to result in inverted bell curves when plotted.

(Insert your name here) RATE OF SPEECH TABLE											
SCALE	<-25	-20	-15	-10	-5	Ideal Rate	+5	+10	+15	+20	> +25
ROS											
SCORE	0	20	40	60	80	100	80	60	40	20	0

TOOLS & TECHNIQUES

THE "UH" FACTOR

This factor is easily calculated by counting the number of "uh's" and "um's" used by the speaker in a one minute period (Use your research assistant to help calculate this.)

There is an inverse relationship between ROS and the UH Factor. In other words, the slower the speaker talks, the more likely they are to use lots of uh's and um's. Sometimes this is a nervous habit -- other times it is filler to help the speaker make it through the presentation.

Use the table on the next page to convert the speakers UH Factor into a score and to determine the best course of action. If you feel that the limited number of categories in the table unfairly score the speaker, feel free to interpolate to determine a more accurate score. It will give you something else to do and your research assistant will be impressed with your mathematical prowess. Even if you do the calculations wrong, the odds are excellent that your neighbor won't know how to interpolate, so they won't notice.

TOOLS & TECHNIQUES

UH Factor	SCORE	DESCRIPTION/ACTION
0	100	This is an experienced speaker. There may be no substance to what they say, but they will say it well. Sit back and enjoy.
0-10	70	Average performer. Probably speaks near your ideal rate. It should be no problem overlooking the uh's and um's.
10-20	30	Unenlightened participants (who have not calculated the UH Factor) will be annoyed but not know why. As the presentation progresses, the speaker's credibility suffers and the ABL climbs. The speaker will be oblivious to the glazed eyes facing them.
20+	0	You are listening to a Flatliner, a Brand New Speaker, or a Last Minute Fill-In. Now that you have started counting the UH Factor, you will be unable to stop. You have three choices -- leave, sleep, or begin holding up cue cards to let the speaker know they are approaching a new UH Factor record (see *Destroying Speaker Confidence*).

TOOLS & TECHNIQUES

VISUAL AID USE

Information is best retained when it is presented several ways, so many speakers utilize visual aids to reinforce a point. The exact number of reinforcements needed varies dramatically from one person to another. Speakers must gauge the audience to determine the right number. Their audience may be largely geniuses who will be annoyed when the information is presented a second time. Or it may be mostly boneheads who begin to grasp the rudimentary concept on the 100th separate illustration (long after the geniuses stormed out of the room).

For purposes of the Speaker Rating Scorecard we shall assume that the ideal number of examples or visual aids is three. This assumption is based on the incredible frequency of three pointed speeches. (Pointless speeches placed second.) Therefore, you should record a score of 50 on the Scorecard for any speaker who uses three ways to illustrate a concept. If they use fewer you may not remember the concept and if they use more you will probably get progressively annoyed. So deduct 15 points from the maximum score of 50 for each example used that is fewer or greater than three.

TOOLS & TECHNIQUES

AVERAGE BOREDOM LEVEL (ABL)

This is a measure of the collective boredom level of the group. It is determined through the following calculation:

$$\left[A^2 \times (N-S) + (C-C_a) \times \frac{IC}{Co} \right] - [ROS + Uh] \times T$$

Where:
A = Quantity of alcohol consumed the previous night
N = Number of hours since the session began
S = Number of hours of sleep the previous night
C = Carbohydrates consumed
Ca = Caffeine consumed
IC = Instructor Charisma (see *Charisma Barometer*)
Co = Complexity of the Subject (see *Topic Excitement Meter*)
R = Rate of Speech (Words per minute)
U = Uh Factor (see *Uh Factor*)
T = Time since last break

TOOLS & TECHNIQUES

As depicted in the graph, this factor generally increases gradually during the morning with an upward curve that gets steeper around lunch. Participants begin to focus at that time on the inadequacy of the continental breakfast and on their mounting Severe Bladder Tension (see *Physical Conditions*).

Following the chicken dish at lunch, the ABL remains high as participants struggle to fight the overwhelming desire to take a nap. Participant boredom tends to drop dramatically just before the end of the day's sessions.

The upward slope and overall range of this factor tend to increase significantly with each successive day as the participant information saturation exceeds maximum capacity.

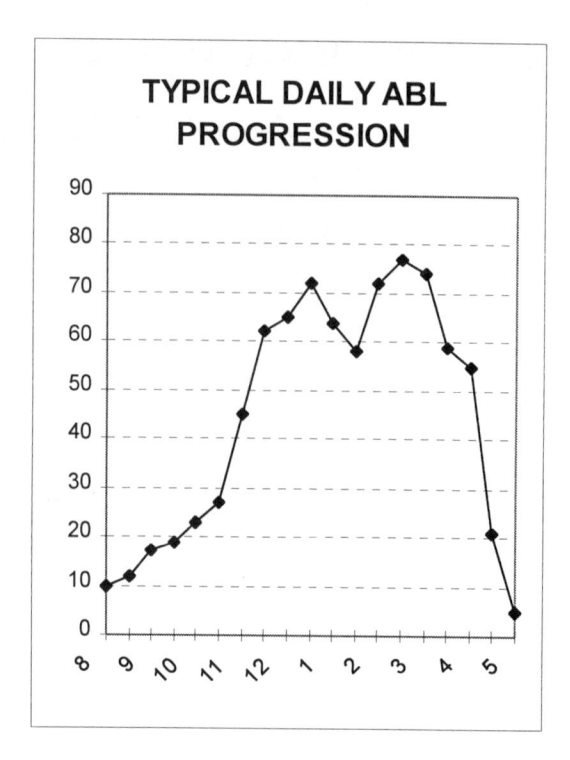

TYPICAL DAILY ABL PROGRESSION

Surviving Seminars:

TOOLS & TECHNIQUES

For purposes of completing the Speaker Rating Scorecard, calculate the ABL at the beginning of the session and again at the end. It will be necessary to gather information from each of the participants to complete the formula. Use the miniature pad of paper supplied by the hotel and pass it around the room with columns for each of the following questions to be filled in by fellow participants:

- How much did you drink last night?
- How many hours did you sleep last night?
- How many grams of carbohydrates have you consumed so far today?
- How many grams of caffeine have you consumed so far today?
- How do you rate this speaker on the Charisma Barometer?
- Where do you rate this subject on the Topic Excitement Meter?
- What score would you give this speaker for their ROS?

When you get the pad back, quickly tabulate the data you have collected and calculate averages for each of the variables in the formula above. If the group is large, distributing several sheets will expedite the process. You might want to bring a laptop computer and build spreadsheets with macros to further expedite the process. Since the clicking keyboard might

TOOLS & TECHNIQUES

annoy fellow participants, consider using a portable bar code reader and providing instructions with the questionnaire on how participants can create their own bar code with a number two pencil.

You should have calculated the remaining variables while you were waiting for the pad to work its way around the room. Double-check your figures. Small mathematical errors in the variables can result in large differences in the final ABL. Repeat this process at the end of the session. Add the beginning and ending scores together and divide by 2 to determine the ABL. Finally, subtract this score from 100 and record the result on the Speaker Rating Scorecard.

TOOLS & TECHNIQUES

TABLETOP GRAVITATION (TTG)

This powerful force is directly proportional to the time since the last break and is inversely related to the Topic Excitement Factor and the Charisma Barometer reading. It can be measured by tabulating the average distance between the heads of participants and tabletops (Head to Table Average Distance (HTAD)).

Although interesting to look at as a snapshot, it is far more meaningful to look at changes in the gravitational force over time. In general, this force tends to increase as the day wears on in much the same fashion as ABL. On occasion, however, a really outstanding speaker can reverse the strengthening trend of Tabletop Gravitation. Therefore, scores for TTG are tied to the percentage change in the HTAD from the beginning of the session to the end. Give the speaker one point for each 1% change in the HTAD. Negative scores are likely. Large positive scores are possible but rare.

To determine the HTAD of fellow participants, follow the steps outlined on the next two pages.

TOOLS & TECHNIQUES

1. Create a chart on a sheet of hotel pad paper with three columns labeled A, B, and C.

2. Cut a vertical slot along the line on the outside border of this page.

3. Estimate the distance in inches from you to the participant you wish to measure. Write this down in column A.

4. Look through the slot in the page at arm's length and count the number of tick marks from the desk to the person's chin. Write the number in column B.

5. Estimate the distance in inches from you to a spot on the chin of the participant you are measuring. Write this value in column C.

6. Repeat for every participant in the room.

7. Calculate the value of B using the formula $B^2 = C^2 - A^2$. Ignore the numbers you wrote in column B as they are irrelevant.

TOOLS & TECHNIQUES

8   Throw away the results since they mean nothing for participants who weren't sitting exactly erect creating a perfect right triangle.

9   Since you have now attracted the attention of almost everyone in the room, go to Plan B. Pass a ruler around the room so that participants can measure the distance exactly. Enter these values in column A of a new table.

10 Repeat the process at the end of the session. Enter these values in column B of the new table.

11 Sum each column. Subtract the column B sum from the column A sum. Divide this figure into the column A sum to determine the percentage change.

Because this process is potentially more interesting than the speaker, it may result in the Hawthorne Effect where the research technique itself impacts the results. Because participants become involved in the process they may arrive with you in Serendipity. Your results will be meaningless but you'll no longer be bored . (This paragraph is dedicated to you Organizational Behaviorists. You know who you are.)

TOOLS & TECHNIQUES

QUANTUM LOGIC LEAP (QL^2)

Inattentive participants often miss these offenses. They occur when the speaker has completely overlooked blatantly obvious facts, which would radically alter the conclusion reached if considered. Give the speaker 10 negative points for each Quantum Logic Leap they successfully present without challenge from the audience.

(Note: Flatliners have a disproportionate chance of scoring well on this measure since many participants have quietly slipped into comas during the presentation and are therefore, somewhat unlikely to catch, much less challenge QL^2's.)

TOOLS & TECHNIQUES

DEAD HORSE FACTOR

Dead Horses are subjects that the speaker (or group) has beaten to death and continues to beat. Some speakers do this because it is the only portion of the material that they are truly prepared to cover. Others permit it to happen because they have no concept of time (which tends to make them unpopular speakers anyway). Still others get so focused on proving a point that they miss the obvious fact that everyone but them has moved on to other activities.

Give the speaker negative 10 points for each subject they continue to discuss after the last breath of life has left the subject. Subtract 1 additional point for each minute they continue to discuss the subject after the horse is dead. You can help cut this short by displaying the Dead Horse Indicator to the speaker or audience (see *Tools & Techniques - Destroying Speaker Confidence*).

TOOLS & TECHNIQUES

TOPIC EXCITEMENT SCORE

Some sessions can have a speaker with Charismetric Pressure off the charts, dazzling audio/visual effects, a mid-morning schedule, moderate climatic conditions that are comfortable for all but a topic with no possibility of generating excitement. These are frequently disguised on the program with clever names to avoid the mass boycott that would result from full disclosure. Sometimes a session scheduled just after lunch with a bad speaker, frigid conditions, and no visual aids can generate a packed house. It's easy to determine an excitement reading for these sessions...it's zero or a perfect 100.

For sessions that fall in the middle, the excitement level they create depends on the individual. There are two commonly accepted ways to measure them. The most obvious is to pass a sheet so everyone can rate the topic from 0 to 100 and calculate an average score. The action of another paper being passed around has the potential, however, of attracting the speaker's attention. They will be offended when the purpose is exposed (as if you were worried about that given all the other things you've already done!).

Less obtrusive, but more involved, is a formula based on observations while you wait for other measurement forms to be returned. Calculate the Participants to Seats Ratio (number of participants divided by the number of available seats). Subtract from it the incidents of Eyelid Droop, the number of participants who leave before the session ends, and the change in Tabletop Gravitation. Though there is a strong correlation between Topic Excitement and a variety other factors, exhausting statistical research proved that these factors provide the most reliable measure of this completely subjective figure.

TOOLS & TECHNIQUES

HAND SIGNALS

With a little practice, you can accomplish amazing things with hand signals and body language. Not only can this help prevent attacks of Cerebral Relocation, but it can also provide entertainment for fellow participants and can be a powerful tool for destroying speaker confidence. You can use real sign language, but it's more fun to create your own with another participant. Here are a few examples to get you started. If you pay close attention, you'll be surprised how many people are already using them.

- **Question Fake** – Quickly lift your hand partially while the speaker is looking. Then stretch when they stop their lecture to entertain your question. Except for those well practiced with excellent timing, this technique works best if you're on the back row.

- **Alternate Question Fake** – Frown visibly and tilt your head slightly to the side when the speaker looks your way. This has the potential, however, to elicit questions from certain types of speakers.

- **"I've heard enough."** – Wiggle your finger gently in your ear.

TOOLS & TECHNIQUES

- **"This stinks!"** – Scratch your nose subtly.

- **"Do you see what I see?"** - Point to your eye and gently nod in the direction of whatever you observed.

- **"I'm preparing to ask some debilitating questions."** – Clear your throat.

- **"This is incredibly boring."** – Fold your fingers up and down as if counting. This indicates you have begun counting ceiling tiles to keep your mind active.

More brazen people who are proficient at signing (or excellent at pretending) can have great fun volunteering to sign for another participant who pretends to be deaf. Simply sign messages that diverge significantly from the speaker's statements or gesture ridiculously. An alternate approach that will quickly end your performance is to scream exactly what the speaker said to the "deaf" person.

TOOLS & TECHNIQUES

DISPLAY, CARE, AND MAINTENANCE OF USELESS BINDER COLLECTIONS

No matter how bulky or heavy the seminar's useless binder, resist the temptation to leave it at the hotel. It can prove immensely useful in securing future conference attendance, impressing subordinates, and annoying jealous co-workers. When you return to the office, this badge of distinction should be displayed prominently on a bookshelf with binders from other seminars. This demonstrates to everyone your level of continued development and application of your newfound knowledge. A large collection also subtly shows your skill at office politics and budgeting.

If you failed to dog-ear pages, underline key points, and jot notes in the binder during the seminar, then you should do this at the airport while you are waiting for the flight that was cancelled or for your luggage to arrive. Failure to do so could undermine your efforts to secure future conference attendance. Be sure to create a nice looking spine label for the binder if the seminar organizers failed to do so. Without the spine label, there is no point in placing the binder on the bookshelf since only the nosiest co-workers will know it is there.

TOOLS & TECHNIQUES

ENSURING FUTURE CONFERENCE ATTENDANCE

The few new ideas you were able to capture when you weren't applying the possible solutions from this book can help you secure attendance at future seminars. The key to this effort is convincing the person that sent you that the money was well spent. To do this you must show how the organization benefited from your attendance at the seminar.

On the return flight, draft a memo to your boss sharing major concepts presented at the seminar and how you will implement them. This memo will probably become part of your next performance evaluation so choose these points carefully. Tasks that closely align with your boss's view of progress are a good idea. Things that are totally within your control are also a good idea. This is because coworkers who stayed home with the boss while you attended the seminar are unlikely to be overwhelmingly receptive to new concepts.

TOOLS & TECHNIQUES

Find occasions to weave key points from the conference into conversations with your boss. You might also pull out the binder from its prominent position on your bookshelf in their presence or copy pages for them that might prove useful. Avoid this sort of grandstanding in front of co-workers as they may launch a lobbying effort to counteract yours.

With the single exception of travel horrors, never mention physical conditions you encountered at the seminar. If a coworker went with you to the seminar, solicit a vow of silence from them about any physical conditions you experienced. This is much easier if you have some evidence regarding their experience at the seminar. It's probably not a good idea either to mention techniques from this book that you applied during the seminar.

GLOSSARY

"I know what they said, but what does it mean?"

GLOSSARY

Alert - A participant condition, which rarely occurs after lunch.

Alumni – These are participants who attended an earlier version of this seminar and returned to share the many ways that the first one was better.

Audience Participation – Technique used by speakers to help participants develop skills for multi-channel processing and inner awareness. By evaluating their own public speaking inadequacies while simultaneously listening for questions directed at them in a high stress environment, participants emerge stronger people but have little content knowledge from the session.

Ballroom – A large sub-dividable room with ugly carpet, neutral walls, a large plastic chandelier, uncomfortable chairs, and bad acoustics.

Beverage Service – Carts or tables of coffee, tea, soft drinks, water, or other beverages designed to increase conditions of Severe Bladder Tension. Frequently accompanied by salty foods, which assist in water retention.

GLOSSARY

Binder – A three-ring folder containing a substantial quantity of documents with no practical purpose outside of the confines of the seminar except to provide substantiation that information was presented.

Book Sale – Table(s) of books by the speakers for those participants who want to further impress their boss by extending seminar related shelf space in their office.

Break – The brief period between sessions when several hundred participants descend upon the five restroom stalls and three courtesy phones to accomplish the things they thought about during the previous session.

Conference Rooms – These are large re-configurable rooms named along a theme that provides geographic direction only to the hotel staff. Similar to salons, but larger.

Cocktail Hour – The part of the seminar during which the greatest volume of meaningful information exchange occurs.

GLOSSARY

Continental Breakfast – A collection of stale bread, sugar-laden treats, and old fruit that the hotel and Seminar Planners set up in the hope that participants will arrive on time for the morning session.

Courtesy Phones – A token number of telephones clustered in a congested area of hallway near the conference rooms. At least one phone is always out of order but not labeled as such.

Feedback – A sheet of cleverly worded questions designed to reinforce the Seminar Planners' opinion of how good the seminar was.

Food – Chicken with rice. Chicken with pasta. Chicken decorated as beef.

Get Acquainted Session – a) a casual reception with alcohol and little or no seating designed to maximize interaction among participants, b) a stress test designed to publicly examine the memory skills of participants.

GLOSSARY

Graduation – Presentation of a worthless but occasionally impressive certificate whose main purpose is to advertise for the seminar.

Group Project – Division of a large group into smaller units to tackle similar or identical tasks. Results of their effort must be presented to the entire group by the most reluctant and ineffective public speaker in the group.

Handout – Preprinted document containing either all of the salient points presented by the speaker or points they intended to discuss.

Hospitality Suite – Hotel room converted with minimal effort into a miniature cocktail lounge to induce inebriation as the vendor/host builds relationships for future sales.

Instructions – Rapid-fire information presented by Seminar Coordinators at the conclusion of sessions to participants who have already packed their writing instruments and paper or who have already left.

GLOSSARY

Jargon - Terms that are highly meaningful to the speaker and seminar groupies, but which send participants searching through the useless binder for a glossary.

Lecturer – Dull speaker.

Lectern – Device used to prop up speaker notes, fix a speaker's location by holding a microphone, and conceal knocking knees of inexperienced speakers.

Manual – Documentation of acceptable methods for doing something. May be contained in the useless binder.

Multimedia Extravaganza – Term used to add promotional sizzle to a slide show, computer presentation, or video. Rarely lives up to the hype.

Name Badge – Used by hotel staff to identify seminar participants (except at a Ritz Carlton where participants are asked to remain anonymous) so they can concentrate on other guests who aren't paying a discounted rate. Also used by participants to confirm identities of people they want to remember.

GLOSSARY

Off-line – Slang for "These people have no business hearing this, so let's discuss it later."

Overhead Projector – Device used to make dull information large but not legible.

Parking Lot – Marker board to capture topics far too comprehensive or controversial for the seminar so that they can be addresses at a later date which never arrives.

Participant List or Guide – Tool for participants to record events and activities from the seminar beside the names and addresses of appropriate participants for future use.

Podium – See Lectern.

Portable Microphone – Device used to make seating strategy more challenging by increasing speaker mobility. Also used to amplify the last two words of paragraph-long questions from audience members.

GLOSSARY

Pre-Registration – Multi-page document to obtain detailed information about the participant for development of mailing lists which may be sold to direct marketers to increase the profitability of the seminar.

Presenter – Speaker who did not develop the concept but who is tasked with conveying it to participants.

Registration – Table with tags arranged in alphabetical order showing participants where to pick up their name badges, useless binders and CPJ (Cheap Plastic Junk) kit. Also a location for confirming the arrival of other participants by checking for the absence of their materials.

Restroom – Facilities to relieve Severe Bladder Tension designed by architects who assumed a controlled number of people would visit them in a controlled manner.

Refreshments – Small food provided during breaks and inside some sessions to promote Severe Bladder Tension and induce sleep related conditions.

GLOSSARY

Salon - Small to medium sized conference room named for some person, place, or thing which provides virtually no clue regarding its physical location.

Schedule - Published document detailing the times, topics, and locations of seminar sessions used by participants to screen out sessions with no obvious value or to determine the length of time to the next break in sessions that appeared to have value.

Seminar Inside Humor - Anecdotes of the seminar personnel, by the seminar personnel, and for the seminar personnel which would annoy non-seminar personnel if they were listening.

Sessions - An expanse of time between breaks during which a transfer of information from speakers to participants is attempted.

Slide Show - Carefully arranged collection of static images to make dull data large.

Speaker – Session leader who attempts to cause information migration from one cranial location to many.

Staff - Employees of the sponsoring organization who always look fresh despite being up 20

GLOSSARY

hours daily making the seminar happen smoothly. They are able to accomplish this because their break schedule is the opposite of yours.

Tour - Extracurricular activities involving large partially filled buses sometimes planned as a diversion from the seminar. Many participants do what they wished had been arranged for the tour instead, accounting for the vacant seats on the busses.

Updates – Announcements by the Seminar Coordinator correcting items that were poorly planned.

Video Monitor - Device used to display video images on a screen that is too small with a speaker that is too loud.

Video Projector - Device used to convert small sharp video images into large impressionistic representations of their former selves on screens large enough for everyone to observe. Surrealism may also be achieved by amplifying the soundtrack from locations away from the screen creating a state of disorientation for viewers.

AFTERWARD

"Finally, something useful!"

AFTERWARD

If you've headed to your first seminar, you may have found this book somewhat disconcerting. You might be a little apprehensive at this point about what you are about to experience. Seasoned seminar survivors probably laughed about some of the same things as they read and recalled their own experiences.

Regardless of which category you fall into, you can use this section of *Surviving Seminars* to get more from your next seminar or conference. Contrary to most of this book, the following pages offer some advice that you might actually want to use.

The advice is grouped into several categories for easy reference and lists are offered in no particular order. If you get nothing else from this section, it should be that your seminar experience can be maximized if you learn to laugh at the nonsense, stay focused on the substance and your goals, and build your list of contacts while there.

AFTERWARD

Overall Advice #1   Laugh.

To get the most from any seminar experience you must maintain a good sense of humor. You are out of your usual surroundings and probably with people you don't know. Things will happen that irritate you. Learn to laugh about them so they don't detract from your learning opportunity.

That's what this book is all about -- not letting the small stuff bother you by seeing how absurd it is. By thinking about the many ludicrous solutions presented elsewhere in this book (You did see them as juvenile pranks that shouldn't be used didn't you?), you can laugh about the problems. And then you can move on to more productive pursuits. Like how to maximize what you get from your seminar.

AFTERWARD

Overall Advice #2 Stay Focused.

Once you learn to identify sources of aggravation and laugh about them, you can focus your attention on the things that are important to you. Here's how you can do that.

Set goals and plan how to achieve them. Before you leave for the seminar, decide what you hope to accomplish. Your time there will be limited and your activities should match your objectives. If you want to learn about topics new to you, then choose sessions that move you toward that goal. If you want to expand your network of contacts, then your approach should increase interaction with groups of people.

Measure your performance. Check off questions as they get answered and goals as you achieve them.

Find ways to use what you learn. While you learn, think about opportunities to apply what you hear. Some applications may not be obvious, but almost everything can be put to use. For example, initially bad experiences provided the inspiration for this book.

Overall Advice #3 Build Contacts.

Seminars are a rare opportunity to find many experts or peers in a single place. Take advantage of that by identifying people you might contact after the seminar. Maximize your opportunities to meet people by carefully managing your schedule and your interaction while there.

Even if your goal is purely to get information and you are an introvert, don't underestimate the value of social interaction at the seminar. You'll be amazed how much you can learn from the post session conversations in casual settings. Participants compare notes on what was said and share their experiences much more freely in that setting. By staying in touch with the people you meet, your opportunity to learn can be extended well beyond the dates of the seminar.

See more about this in the advice about participants.

AFTERWARD

Overall Advice #4 Provide Honest Feedback.

Whether you liked the seminar or didn't, provide honest feedback on the review forms. Most trainers and conference planners are genuinely interested in improving their performance so they need to know what didn't work well. Be fair, though, and let them know what you liked. You like to receive sincere praise and so do they.

After the seminar, give honest feedback to the people that sent you. They want to know that the money was well spent. Don't be afraid to say it wasn't. More about this later.

AFTERWARD

Advice about the Travel Experience

Try to find a silver lining in everything that happens. If nothing else, the situation gives you material for Travel Horror Story competitions. Or material for stories to tell your grandchildren someday about how tough you had it.

Think about how the situation could be worse and then rejoice that it's not. Sometimes just thinking about ridiculous possibilities can make you feel better. Smiling and sharing those thoughts with other angry road warriors can ease tension.

Don't take out your frustration on innocent parties. It's rare that someone intends to cause problems for you. Treat people courteously and they will usually respond in kind. Address unmet expectations with that service provider. But don't act like they fulfilled their life ambition by making your life miserable. You might inspire them to do so.

Sometimes it's best to just sit down for a few minutes, close your eyes and take some deep breaths. Then systematically think through your options and work out plans for solving the problem. A few calm minutes may save you hours of stress and effort.

AFTERWARD

Eat, drink and sleep like you would at home. Drink lots of water, even if you don't at home. You need to be at your best and changes in these behaviors will affect how you feel and what you are able to do.

Consider potential "disasters" when making your travel plans. Arrive earlier than you have to -- just in case. Allow time afterward to explore contacts or to gather your thoughts.

Take advantage of the travel time to think and to plan what you will do when you reach your destination. Remember how rare it is to have that much time away from the phone.

AFTERWARD

Advice about Participants

Focus on what they have to offer instead of what annoys you. You will get far more from the seminar if you open your mind to new or different approaches. This is more difficult if you only see the idiosyncrasies of people who have much to offer. Exaggerate their "flaws" dramatically in your mind. Laugh to yourself and move on.

Many of your fellow participants are experiencing the same anxieties and discomforts. They may be there for various reasons, but all of you can benefit by sharing the experience. Each of you arrives at the seminar with unique knowledge that becomes more valuable when pooled. Therefore, there is a direct link between your interaction with other people and what you have accomplished when the seminar is complete. Here are some ways that you can maximize your exposure to people and concepts.

Move around. Sit in different parts of the room(s) for each session. Sit beside at least one new person each session.

AFTERWARD

Vow to make at least one new friend each day even if you know many of the people at the seminar. Don't get caught in the trap of meeting someone the first day and hanging out with them the entire time.

Introduce yourself to the people sitting next to you at each session. Learn something unique about them. Write down their name, where they are from, and the unique thing you learned about them.

Volunteer as a group leader. It's an opportunity to polish your leadership and speaking skills.

Take advantage of casual group gatherings in the bar or restaurants. You can learn about other perspectives on the material and get anecdotal information about applying the new knowledge. Limit alcohol intake and how late you stay. The quality of information tends to deteriorate as the evening progresses.

AFTERWARD

Advice about Presentations and Presenters

Focus on the concepts being presented and not the flaws in presentation. This may not be easy but it is important. Developing your ability to concentrate on substance regardless of the form will pay rich dividends both at work and in your personal life.

Be glad that you are not the one on stage. It's easy to be critical from the audience. Presenting information on any subject to increasingly savvy and skeptical audiences is not easy. If you don't think so, then you should try it. You'll be far more sympathetic.

Do your homework. Come to the presentation armed with at least basic knowledge of the topic. Consider questions that might be posed to the audience and develop answers to them. Prepare questions for which you seek answers. Check them off as they are covered. Explore them further with the presenter or participants if you remain unclear.

Constantly look for ways to apply the concepts being presented and write them down. Look beyond the obvious to illogical or even implausible approaches. You'll remember concepts better if you find ways they can fit in your situation. And you'll have a head start putting the seminar to use when you get home.

AFTERWARD

Take advantage of opportunities like group meals to discuss topics with speakers. You can obtain additional information in a less threatening situation than in front of the entire group and this can offer extraordinary networking possibilities.

Interject support for the speaker's statements or additional detail if you have some expertise on the subject. The speaker will appreciate the support and the break from speaking. So will the audience. This is particularly true if the speaker is inexperienced.

Avoid using sarcasm. Though entertaining, it doesn't serve you well in this setting, particularly if you seek to find a new job from someone in the crowd. It can also be badly misinterpreted by people who don't view things the same way as you.

Provide honest feedback. Say thank you when the presentation was good and/or provided you with inspirations. Offer constructive suggestions about how the presentation could be improved. If you know someone who could make weak visuals stronger, offer them as a potential source. The speaker and your contact will appreciate the referral.

AFTERWARD

Advice about Putting It To Use

The seminar investment will be in vain if you don't put your new knowledge to use when you return home. Use the travel time to prioritize the applications you jotted down during the seminar. Think about how you will communicate and implement them.

Don't forget to consider co-workers who didn't get to go when you build the plan. They may be jealous and resist changes as a result. Find ways to involve them. Share concepts with them rather than descriptions of the great time you had. They may expand on your thoughts and find even better applications for the ideas. Be receptive.

Discuss your thoughts with your boss. Thank them for sending you and share the positive things you gained from the experience.

Take advantage of your new contacts from the seminar and keep in touch with them to continue the exchange of information, to communicate progress on implementing things learned at the seminar, and to build a network for future resume' exchange.

ABOUT THE AUTHOR

During nearly 20 years of management roles in the Financial Services industry, Randy Segler has attended countless seminars and conferences. The patterns he observed and his ability to find humor in them provided the inspiration for *Surviving Seminars: A Humorous Self-Help Guide*. This book in turn provided the inspiration for the *Surviving Stuff Series*. This series helps people cope with life's frustrations by helping them see the humor that surrounds us. It covers a variety of topics from seminars to travel to raising children. Segler's unique style helps us laugh about ludicrous solutions to problems that seem smaller when his humorous style puts them in perspective.

To contact him, write in care of The Surviving Stuff Company, P.O. Box 15655, Panama City, FL 32406-5655 or send email to rsegler@survivingstuff.com.

In progress are guides on how to survive:

Business Travel . Camping . College . Dinner Parties . Family Gatherings

Family Vacations . Holidays . Home Construction/Remodeling

House Guests . Management . Pets . Reunions . System Enhancements

The Business World . The Great Outdoors . Teenagers . Toddlers

Send in your ideas!

If you've seen humor in a situation and it helped you survive, send in your idea. You'll be recognized if your idea is included in a future book. Just answer this simple question:

"I survived _____ by _____."

Include your name, address, and a phone number (note whether it is a daytime or an evening number) so we can confirm anything we don't understand and make sure you get credit for the contribution in the appropriate guide.

Send your suggestions by mail to Randy Segler, c/o The Surviving Stuff Company, P.O. Box 15655, Panama City, FL 32406-5655 or by email to rsegler@survivingstuff.com or submit them via the Internet at www.survivingstuff.com.

Visit

www.survivingstuff.com

for more information from or about

The Surviving Stuff Company.